THE
WOMEN'S
CENTURY

THE
WOMEN'S
CENTURY

A celebration of changing roles

Mary Turner

the national archives

First edition published in 2003
Paperback edition published in 2006 by

The National Archives
Kew, Richmond
Surrey, TW9 4DU, UK
www.nationalarchives.gov.uk

The National Archives was formed when the Public Record Office and
Historical Manuscripts Commission combined in April 2003

Reprinted 2004

A catalogue record for this book is available from the British Library

ISBN-10: 1 903365 84 8
ISBN-13: 978 1 903365 84 7

Jacket front painting by Clement Serveau in *L'Illustration*, 1931
front thumbnails Christabel Pankhurst, 1906; Maureen Geary-Andrews
in WRAF uniform, 1966; Princess Diana, 1997
back poster, *The Broads*, advertising expensive holidays, 1926
left flap Welsh recruits to Women's Army Auxiliary Corps, 1917 *right flap* Mary Turner,
2003 *Title page* Margot Williams (left), her daughter-in-law, Isobel Shelley (right), with
granddaughter, Diana Shelley (centre), Covent Garden. *c.*1945.

Pages designed and typeset by Carnegie Publishing, Lancaster, Lancashire
Printed and bound in China on behalf of Compass Press Ltd

Contents

As this mid-century recruitment poster indicates, nursing was considered women's work. It was thought that the caring aspects of the job made it an ideal preparation for later marriage and motherhood – for many years it was one of the few professions that girls were actively encouraged to enter.

Foreword

Jenni Murray

No matter how much you think you know about the terrible injustices suffered by women in the past and the extraordinary progress that was achieved within such a short time, there is always something new to shock you or make you burst with pride. Sixteen years presenting Woman's Hour on Radio 4 has meant confronting these horrors and celebrating the advances day after day, but I can still burn with fury at Caroline Norton's experiences in the early part of the nineteenth century. Married to a drunkard and wife beater, she had no access to her children when she escaped. She fought the law and won a small victory, but the right for a separated or divorced woman to see her children wasn't fully granted until 1873.

The story of the suffragettes is one of strength and bravery in the face of violent opposition. There was the brutality of forcible feeding, the constant sexual harassment and even, on Black Friday, sexual assault by the police. There was a law that stated women were not 'persons' and a politician who believed women were not fully human. Nevertheless the fight for the vote continued and the campaigners managed to retain an admirable sense of headline grabbing humour, dropping thousands of leaflets from an airship and posting themselves to the Prime Minister! I've always found my blood boils whenever a young woman asks me 'When were women given the vote?' We weren't 'given' the vote, we fought like tigers for it and won.

This book is a brilliant record of the century in which the gender landscape of this country altered beyond all recognition. It marks every important political development in the battle for women to be recognised as equal human beings to men, with the same rights to equal pay, education and access to jobs from which a hundred years ago we were excluded. The great leaps forward and the little steps back are recorded — more than a hundred women in Parliament, but they call them 'Blair's Babes', for instance — but, most importantly, Mary Turner includes the human stories of individual women who suffered terrible discrimination and took on the establishment to change the world.

When I wrote my own book, *That's My Boy!*, I pointed out how little the two sexes know and understand of the history that brought us to the position we are in now: where equal numbers of boys and girls are being trained for the professions; where many more girls are beginning to see engineering or nuclear physics as a possible option; and where it's no longer possible for boys to assume that they'll never need to learn how the cooker and the washing machine function or that childcare is women's work. I suggested a new subject for schools. Sex education, I argued, should be abolished and the technicalities of reproduction, contraception and the prevention of disease should be included in biology, in the cool atmosphere of the laboratory. Then all pupils, boys and girls, should have gender education where they learn the story of the relations between men and women. This volume would provide the perfect textbook; the history of a period which turned the world, quite rightly, upside down.

Preface

As a woman living in Britain in the twenty-first century, I realise that I have a great deal to be thankful for when I compare my life with that of my female ancestors. Today women have much to celebrate. They not only have the vote but they have proved that no position in government is too high for them. Although they are still in the minority in Parliament their numbers are growing and they are no longer confined to areas of social welfare when they serve in government. They have won a number of legal freedoms, including the right to be considered as separate and equal individuals within marriage. In theory at least, the law protects them from discrimination and sexual harassment.

At the start of the twenty-first century women are accepted in all professions: they can be astronauts, bankers, judges, priests or anything else that they choose. They have adopted 'masculine' clothing, and jeans and trouser suits are now as acceptable as dresses and skirts. They even participate in the 'masculine' sports of football, rugby and boxing though, for obvious reasons, in these they do not compete with men. There seems no limit to what they can achieve. Women have scaled Everest, sailed single-handedly around the world and made successful expeditions to the Poles.

In Britain we have become used to girls out-performing boys at school and at university. We are accustomed to women being open about their sexuality and to seeing pregnant women proudly displaying their 'bumps'. We are also used to hearing about 'ladettes', hard-drinking, housework-hating women who act as their brothers do on a 'lads' night out'. Largely as a consequence of the blurring of gender roles and changes in expectations, just as the number of women entering 'male' professions has increased so too has the number of women going to prison for crimes of violence.

One hundred years ago all of this would have been unthinkable. Yet the remarkable story of how twentieth century women challenged their perceived inferiority and fought their way to a near equality is not widely known. For the greater part of the twentieth century women's history was not a subject considered worthy of academic study and women were rarely mentioned in school history lessons. Even in later years, many schools, if they bothered at all, taught 'women's history' as a short unit as though it were a separate subject and not a part of 'real' history. As a result few women, and even fewer men, have learned much about the struggles and achievements of women in the past.

During my years as a history teacher in a girls' school, I did what I could to bring aspects of women's lives into the main topics of the history curriculum; I found that students were often surprised and fascinated by what they learned. Several women have told me they wished that they had learned more about women's history while they were at school. This illustrated book aims to provide those who would like to know more with an overview of the changes that took place in women's lives over the twentieth century. It charts the story of the countless women whose battles, whether as part of a larger movement or as an individual effort, have brought us the freedoms we enjoy at the start of the twenty-first century.

While researching this book I became aware of how rich and varied women's experiences have been over the decades. Change affected them in different ways and at different times depending on their individual circumstances. This became truer as the century wore on and women gained more choice and greater control over their lives. The more I read and the more I talked to women, the more I realised the impossibility of doing justice to all their experiences. Yet their stories deserve to be told. With this in mind I have included anecdotes from the lives of ordinary women as well as the more famous, although I have not had enough space to include as many of their stories as I would have liked. In deciding who to profile in each chapter I have, in most cases, chosen those who, whether directly or indirectly, have had an impact on other women's lives. Faced with what seemed an impossible number of women to chose from, my choice was often guided by personal preference.

In 1946 Dorothy L. Sayers wrote that 'the fundamental thing is that women are more like men than anything else in the world. They are human beings ... This is the equality claimed and the fact that is persistently evaded and denied'. More than half a century later her words still ring true, and until both men and women are able to live their lives free from gender constraints, equality will not be achieved. Yet women in Britain today have more choice and more freedom than at any other time in their history. This book is intended to celebrate the struggles, the work and the achievements of the women of the twentieth century which made this possible.

Acknowledgements

First I have to thank Sheila Knight, the editor who commissioned this book, for her unfailing patience and encouragement – without her the book would never have been conceived, let alone written. Thanks too to the publishing team at the National Archives, especially those involved in the picture research. A special thanks to Diana Shelley, my copy editor, whose contribution to this book, thanks to our many conversations and her wide knowledge and interest in the subject, went far beyond copy-editing. Any mistakes that remain, however, are my responsibility. Thanks too to the research staff of the National Archives, in particular to Sheila Gopaulen for pointing me in the direction of the Second World War material on women from the West Indies.

I would also like to thank the many women who discussed the decades and shared their stories with me, including those who wish to remain anonymous. Thanks also to June Cross for suggesting Rosalind Franklin as a suitable subject to profile and Sally Cornwell for the material from *Vanity Fair* used in the chapter on the 1970s. I have to thank Vanessa and Andrew Webster for the use of their country cottage at a crucial time in the writing of this book and Yarmila Kos whose ministrations warded off incipient repetitive strain injury. I would also like to thank the staff of 'Lindys' in Mill Hill, especially Rose and Jan, who kept me well supplied with tea and encouragement as I scribbled in a corner of the café.

A special thanks must go to my family and friends for their constant support and their patience with me while I put my social life on hold as the deadline approached. I would also like to thank friends and colleagues in the Women Writers' Network. Their advice and encouragement, especially when I first started writing, has been invaluable. Last, but not least, I have to thank my partner David Cameron who, while I was writing this book, put up with research material encroaching into all areas of our home and my demands for a television-free abode. His strides towards becoming a 'new man' are much appreciated. I would also like to thank him for reading several chapters. His evident surprise at finding himself interested in this story of women, despite being, in his words, 'a Scottish male chauvinist', increased my confidence that this was a story that needed be told.

Dedication

This book is dedicated to the memory of: my late mother, Alexandra Marie Reilly (née Wakim), who inspired and encouraged my independence; my late father, Joseph Henry Reilly, who encouraged my love of history and literature; and my late brother, Bernard Joseph Reilly, who, while we were very young, inadvertently turned me into a life-long feminist by telling me that, although I was the eldest, had we been members of the royal family, I would have been last in line because I was only a girl.

A woman's place

Man to command and woman to obey — all else confusion.

TENNYSON

'A woman's place is in the home', or so goes the proverb that for centuries has been accepted as a truth as fixed as any of the Ten Commandments. Before the late nineteenth century, when there was little alternative, few women dared challenge the concept. Indeed, for those obliged by poverty to work in appalling conditions in factories or in domestic service, the chance to stay at home was a dream they could only aspire to. Throughout the nineteenth century a woman was generally regarded as an inferior creature, one who was ruled by her emotions and therefore unreliable and unpredictable. Her role in life was that of a wife and mother and her sole function was to perpetuate the race. As a result, a woman unable to find a husband was an object of pity and often derision.

Life held few opportunities for the majority of women born before the twentieth century and marriage was what most women aspired to. It represented an escape from the parental home and it brought a measure of financial security. For single women without money of their own, the future could be bleak. For most of the nineteenth century, a single woman was financially dependent on her father or male relatives. There were few exceptions. It was rare for a woman to earn enough to keep herself; women's wages were kept low because it was assumed that men would support them. With little opportunity to earn a living, an unmarried woman faced an uncertain future when her parents died. If she had no relatives willing or able to help she could easily end up in the workhouse or worse. In the early nineteenth century, after her father died, and before her writing provided her with an income, Jane Austen, her mother and sister were all dependent on her brother's charity to provide them with a home.

Expectations

Until well into the twentieth century, a woman's fate was largely determined by her class and family circumstances. Throughout the nineteenth century, the ideal situation, one that even the poorest would aspire to, was for a man to support his wife and family. Daughters would stay at home, kept by their father, until they married. Because women were considered frail creatures needing protection, they were expected to spend most of their time indoors. Single women were only allowed to leave the safety of their home if they were accompanied by a chaperone. While at home they were encouraged to occupy themselves with 'womanly' pursuits and those accomplishments that would help them attract a husband. They were not expected to do anything more serious, as intellectual women were thought to frighten off would-be suitors. Any woman that tried to break away from this stultifying existence would meet fierce resistance, as Florence Nightingale (see p. 9) discovered.

The Victorian notion that women were weak creatures was a self-fulfilling prophecy. The ideal of femininity was of a languid, pale, subservient creature. Encouraged to sit around in a stuffy house and made to wear tight corsets that displaced their internal organs, it is little wonder that some women fainted at the least sign of stress. As well as suffering from the restrictions of their clothing, it is likely that much of the poor health of middle and upper class women was caused by lack of fresh air and exercise, and by depression caused by boredom. It's interesting, however, that the very people who saw their wives and daughters as frail creatures thought nothing of asking their female servants to work a sixteen hour day, much of it involving hard physical labour, with little or no rest.

OPPOSITE
In 1896, when this photograph of Miss Harold was taken, women in the upper classes had little to look forward to other than making a good marriage. Once they were of marriageable age they were launched into 'society' and encouraged to attend a number of balls and other functions in the hope of attracting a suitable husband.

Isabella Bishop (née Bird) who, in 1892, became the first woman to be made a fellow of the Royal Geographical Society, is a classic example of how debilitating life as a respectable spinster could be. Born in 1831, Isabella – who did not marry until she was forty-nine – was for many years a typical Victorian spinster. The daughter of a clergyman, she was so plagued with ill health that her doctor recommended sea travel. Her many ailments included 'neuralgia, pain in my bones, pricking like pins and needles in my limbs, excruciating nervousness, exhaustion, inflamed eyes, sore throat, swelling of the glands behind my ears, stupidity'. Yet as her book *A Lady's Life in the Rocky Mountains* shows, once she was freed from the restrictions and expectations of Victorian society, her ailments were forgotten. Her book makes entertaining reading. She endured the hardship and primitive conditions of frontier California without complaint. Her illnesses only recurred when she returned from her travels and was once again cast in the role of respectable spinster.

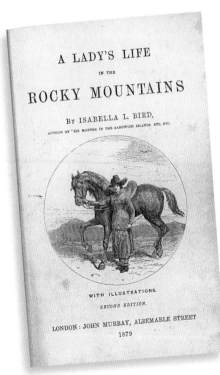

The title page of *A Lady's Life in the Rocky Mountains* by Isabella L. Bird, 1879. Her book was based on letters that she wrote to her sister while she was travelling abroad. It is difficult to imagine what her sister would have made of Isabella's many adventures – especially her friendship with her rough and tough male guide who went by the name of 'Mountain Jim'.

Although the restrictions of domestic life irked many women, to be able to stay at home was little short of a luxury for others. As soon as they were old enough, girls from poor families were sent out to work to supplement the family income. When her family fell on hard times, Annie Kenney, later a prominent suffragette (see profile, p. 20), was sent to work part-time in a textile mill. She was only 10 years old. Apart from in areas like Lancashire, where the textile factories were the largest employers of women, the majority of women worked as domestic servants. Sending out a daughter as a live-in servant was a great help to a poor family as it meant one less mouth to feed. Though in most areas domestic service was considered a cut above factory work, the work was physically demanding, the hours long, and it was poorly paid. It is not surprising that most female servants looked forward to marriage and a home of their own.

Although marriage was an escape from a life in service, many women found they had exchanged one form of drudgery for another. As well as having to do the all cooking and cleaning herself, a woman would have to face the ordeal of almost constant child bearing; families of a dozen, and more, children were common among the poor before the twentieth century. If, for whatever reason, her husband did not bring enough money home she would be forced to find work. Taking in laundry or doing piecework at home was badly paid, but a man would rarely countenance the alternative – a wife who went out to work was a tacit admission that he was unable to provide for his family.

This photograph illustrating slum conditions in the cities was taken in 1892. Women had a difficult time coping in these conditions yet they could be prosecuted for neglecting their children, even though their poverty, poor housing and lack of clean water made it impossible for them to keep them clean and well fed.

Women's legal status

Until the late nineteenth century, a woman not only belonged in the home; she belonged to her menfolk. A father could dictate to his daughters, a husband to his wife. The only women with a measure of independence were wealthy widows or single women with money of their own. Many women married men who treated them well, but for those who did not the law offered very little protection. For most of the nineteenth century, a man had total control over his wife. He had the right to force her to live with him and his conjugal rights entitled him to have sexual intercourse with her whether she was willing or not.

At the start of Queen Victoria's reign, a married woman had no separate existence in law. She was, in effect, her husband's property, and everything she owned, right down to the clothes she wore, became his on their marriage. Any money she earned was also legally his. A feckless husband would be well within his rights if he took his wife's earnings and spent the lot on drinking, gambling or on other women. A woman had no alternative but to accept his behaviour: divorce was not an option and her property remained his even if she subsequently left him.

In the mid 1830s, when Caroline Norton (see box) decided she wanted a divorce, she found it impossible. Until the middle of the nineteenth century, the only way to get a divorce was by an act of Parliament. It was a slow and expensive process and only available to men, usually on the grounds of a wife's adultery. As married women did not officially exist as a separate entity apart from their husbands, they were unable to divorce them. Even after the Matrimonial Causes Act of 1857 gave women the right to a divorce, the law still favoured men.

Until well into the twentieth century, although a man could divorce his wife for adultery, a woman did not have the same right. The reason for the difference in treatment came from the belief that men had natural impulses which women did not have. As a result, his adultery, though regrettable, could not be grounds for divorce as it was due to a natural impulse. A man's infidelity, therefore, was acceptable in law. An unfaithful woman, however, was treated with the utmost revulsion. As she could not blame her natural instincts for any indiscretion, her infidelity was considered a sign of depravity. The merest suspicion of adultery could bring ruin to a woman and her family. Caroline Norton's reputation never recovered after her husband accused her of adultery, even though the courts declared her innocent. No such scandal attached to Lord Melbourne, the man accused with her.

Because of society's double standards, a woman needed to prove cruelty in addition to adultery before she could divorce her husband – though, as a man was allowed to beat his wife, any beating she received would have to be severe indeed before she could cite it in a divorce case. In the nineteenth century wife beating was legal and acceptable, provided the stick he used was no thicker than his thumb. Even Queen Victoria condoned violence towards women, remarking that Lady Amberley 'deserved a good whipping' for daring to make a speech in public in favour of giving women the vote.

A parliamentary report published in *The Times*, dated 18 March 1853, gives some indication of the attitude towards women in Queen Victoria's reign. It reported that, during a debate in the House of Commons, a Mr Fitzroy stated that under English law a woman was worth less than poodle dogs or a Skye terrier.

According to *The Times* his conclusion came from a comparison of punishments imposed by the courts. It reported that 'any man may, at his pleasure, kick, bruise, beat, knock down, and stamp upon' a woman and the fine was a quarter of that for stealing a dog. Worse still, if the fine was unpaid, the crime of viciously beating a woman would bring a two-month prison sentence with hard labour, whereas the theft of a dog brought the much harsher sentence of six months in prison with hard labour. He went on to suggest that women should be classified as animals so

The case of Caroline Norton

Caroline Norton's story illustrates how dependent and vulnerable women were in the nineteenth century. Even those of the privileged upper classes with influential friends were powerless in the face of the harsh laws that discriminated against them.

Like most upper class women of the time, Caroline married for the financial security a husband would provide. Her decision was a terrible mistake. Her husband, George Norton, had lied about his financial situation and, at a time when a man was expected to keep his wife, Caroline was forced to supplement the family income by her writing. She grew to despise her husband and did not bother to hide her feelings. They had widely differing political views and Norton's usual response to Caroline's opinions was to beat her. He was so violent that on more than one occasion others had to intervene to save her from serious injury. After one severe beating she suffered a miscarriage. Although Caroline left her husband when he was at his most violent, she felt obliged to return to the family home in order to be with her children.

After one quarrel, Norton locked her out of their home and accused her of adultery. Although the courts cleared her of the charge, he refused to let her see the children. At that time women had no right to their children – in law they belonged to their father, who had total control over them and could, if he wished, take them away from his wife and place them in the care of his mistress. Norton also cheated Caroline out of money left to her in trust and she was powerless to do anything about it. Even after they were separated, the income from her writing was legally his.

Caroline had some political influence through her powerful friends and she campaigned relentlessly to get the law on child custody changed. The changes she proposed were cautious and allowed a woman who was innocent of adultery to have custody of her children under the age of seven and access to children under sixteen. Her proposals became law in 1839 with the passing of the Custody of Infants Act. This was the first of the laws that would improve the status of women. Caroline continued to campaign for reform in the laws regarding married women, but had to wait until the 1857 Matrimonial Causes Act before she saw any further change. The right to see their children was not extended to all separated and divorced women until 1873.

The Jackson case

A report in *The Times* dated 23 April 1891, on the notorious Jackson case, shows just how bad the situation could be for a woman before the law was changed. In the late 1880s Mrs Jackson left her husband because of his behaviour towards her and her family, and because she believed he only wanted her for her money. Although he took legal proceedings against her and demanded that she return, she repeatedly refused to live with him. In 1889 he kidnapped her. With the help of two men, he grabbed her as she was coming out of church and bundled her into a waiting carriage.

Badly bruised and shaken by the incident, she was taken to his house where she was made a prisoner and not allowed to see her family or friends. She was kept under lock and key, her mail was censored and she was constantly watched. Escape was impossible. According to the report, Mrs Jackson claimed that Blackburn's police superintendent visited her but said that he could not interfere. Her friends managed to get the case to court where it became a test case on the question of whether a man had the right to force his wife to live with him. The case was eventually decided in Mrs Jackson's favour and since 1891 women have had the right to leave their husbands.

that they could be better protected under the Cruelty to Animals Act. Whether Mr Fitzroy was seriously concerned about the treatment of women or whether he was simply being flippant is unclear. However, the report does reveal how badly the law protected women at that time.

Exceptions to the rule

Throughout history there have been strong women who have resisted the stereotypes of their time and broken free of society's expectations. Some, like Joan of Arc, suffered for their actions: she was burnt as a witch for daring to take up a man's role. Elizabeth I held onto her crown and ruled the country in turbulent times in spite of the many intrigues against her. She refused to marry, knowing that if she did she would lose her power. But in most cases the efforts and successes of individuals in earlier times did little or nothing to advance the cause of women.

The efforts of women in the nineteenth century, however, had a more lasting effect. Many strove, not for personal gain or achievement, but to right the many injustices suffered by women. Numerous campaigns were fought and won during Queen Victoria's reign. As well as changes in the laws on the custody of children (see the case of Caroline Norton, p. 7), women's determined and persistent campaigning led to a series of laws that gradually improved a married woman's financial position. In 1870 a married woman was allowed to retain £200 of her own earnings. The biggest improvement, however, came in 1882 when she was granted the same rights to her property as a single woman.

In some cases, wider opportunities for women were created by an individual's refusal to conform to society's expectations. When Florence Nightingale rejected the comfortable but empty existence of an upper class woman and announced that she wished to go into nursing, her parents were horrified. At that time nursing was not regarded as a respectable profession and, with the exception of nurses attached to religious orders, female nurses were seen as slovenly drunks who were little better than whores. Although she faced strong opposition from her family, Florence persisted with her ambition, and with the support of powerful friends she achieved her aims. After her time in the Crimea she continued to work to improve the status of nurses. She founded a school of nursing and wrote books on the subject. Her rebellion not only gave her the freedom to do something worthwhile, but led to the creation of a new occupation for middle class women.

The Victorians portrayed Florence Nightingale as the 'lady with the lamp' to fit their sentimental view of women as the self-sacrificing and nurturing sex. The image played down her real skills of organisation and fund-raising, as these were not considered to be feminine attributes. The woman who better fitted the description of a 'nurturing angel' was Mary Seacole, an extraordinary nurse from Jamaica, who had many years' experience of successfully treating cholera and other tropical diseases. When her offer to join the nurses sent to the Crimea was turned down, she set off on her own, undaunted by the rejection which, as her book *Wonderful Adventures of Mrs Seacole in Many Lands* shows, she suspected was 'because my blood flowed beneath a skin somewhat duskier than theirs'.

In the Crimea, she opened a store and boarding house she called the British Hotel. On the ground floor she ran a canteen where soldiers could eat and drink and on the first floor she set up a place for the sick and wounded. To the men at the front she was a heroine. She thought nothing of going out onto the battlefield to tend to soldiers while the battle was still raging. William H. Russell, correspondent to *The Times*, wrote about her bravery and devotion.

While nursing could be accepted by the Victorians as being within a woman's capability, the idea of a woman becoming a doctor was a much harder pill for them to swallow. The first British woman doctor, Elizabeth Garrett Anderson, found the medical establishment fiercely resistant to women entering the profession; no British medical schools would admit women to their examinations. In spite of this ban she managed to qualify as a doctor by exploiting a loophole in the system. In 1865 she sat the Apothecaries Hall examination, which entitled her to register as a doctor.

After her success, the loophole was firmly closed and women were barred from the examination. Once she qualified, Elizabeth Garrett Anderson concentrated on her medical practice. It was left to another pioneering woman, Sophia Jex-Blake, to carry on the fight to get women accepted into medical schools. It was a difficult battle and even after she had succeeded, it was a long time before women were welcomed into the profession. By the beginning of the twentieth century around 200 women had become doctors but other professions, such as law and accountancy, were still closed to them.

Women's education

The resistance to women entering the professions stemmed partly from the view of them as shallow, flighty creatures, incapable of logical or serious thought. In the eighteenth century Lord Chesterfield had described women as being 'children of a larger growth: they have an entertaining tattle, and sometimes wit; but for solid, reasoning good sense, I never knew in my life one that had it'. This attitude held sway well into the next century with some men claiming that educating women was dangerous to their health. It was believed that women's bodies were too frail and their brains too weak to take the strain of learning, and some held the view that education would impair a woman's ability to reproduce thereby endangering the future of the race.

Until the second half of the nineteenth century a girl's education was not taken seriously. Upper and middle class girls were educated at home by a governess. As they were not expected to achieve anything other than a good marriage, their education was designed to make them into 'accomplished women' who would grace a future husband's home. Young women were expected to be entertaining companions. They were taught to dance, to sing and play the piano, to draw and paint in watercolours, to do fine needlework and embroidery, to recognise countries on a globe and speak at least a little of a foreign language. In case all these accomplishments went to their heads, they were also taught etiquette, modesty and how to move gracefully. One of their most important lessons was to learn to listen attentively whenever a man spoke to them.

Working class girls received little or no education. They were expected to learn all they needed at home by helping their mothers. A few girls went to the charity schools that were set up in the eighteenth century, where they learned domestic skills and how to read. Few girls were taught writing or arithmetic. The records of Finedon Charity School, which are held in the National Archives (C 115/72), show that the girls' 'education' was in fact a preparation for a life as a domestic servant. Only a few of the brightest girls were taught to 'cast accounts' and to write. Although the records of Finedon Charity School date from the eighteenth century, little changed in these schools until the 1870s. Other girls

OPPOSITE
Housewifery lessons under the London School Board in 1893. At that time social mobility was restricted and even highly intelligent girls born to working class families had little option but to go into service. The alternative, factory work, was usually regarded with even less favour.

A LESSON IN WASHING.

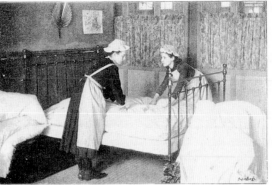

MAKING A BED.

LAYING AND LIGHTING A FIRE.

A LESSON IN HOUSEWIFERY.

DRYING LESSON, WITH KINDERGARTEN CLOTHES, POSTS, AND PEGS.

IRONING.

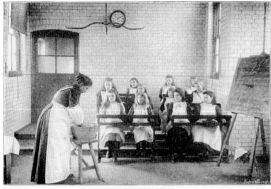

WASHING.

MIXING STARCH.

learnt to read at Sunday schools. Although poor girls rarely learnt to write, they were taught to read so that they could read the bible and other good works.

In education, as in other areas, Victorian women campaigned for change. They wanted girls to be as well educated as their brothers, believing that a good education was vital if women were to be taken seriously. Another compelling reason for educating women was the imbalance in the population. From the second part of the nineteenth century, women outnumbered men. It became clear that as marriage wouldn't be an option for all women, some would need to earn their living. To improve their chances of a gaining employment as a governess or nurse they needed an education.

In the second half of the nineteenth century, a number of academic schools for girls were opened. Although they met with some initial resistance, they were soon accepted. At Cheltenham Ladies College girls were taught science and mathematics,

These colliery girls, photographed in 1900 at Wigan Junction Colliery, near Wigan, would have received little beyond the most basic education. Few people at the turn of the century thought that educating working class girls was worthwhile.

The Contagious Diseases Acts

Throughout the Victorian period a woman was expected to be the moral superior of a man. Good women, it was thought, would keep men, who were at the mercy of their natural instincts, on the straight and narrow. As a woman was expected to be chaste, she was kept in ignorance of sexual matters until she was about to be married. At that point she learned that her duty as a wife required her to endure the 'attentions' of her husband in order to please him. Even after marriage a 'pure' woman was kept in ignorance of the seedier side of life. When Josephine Butler started to campaign on behalf of 'fallen' women, she shocked Victorian society. As a respectable married woman, she was not supposed to know anything about the evils of prostitution, let alone discuss them in public.

Her most successful campaign was against the Contagious Diseases Acts. These were passed in 1866 and 1868 by a government worried about the spread of venereal diseases amongst men in the armed services. The Acts were applied in the major ports and garrison towns of the country. Under the law any woman suspected of being a common prostitute could be taken by the police and forced to undergo a medical examination, with surgical instruments, to check whether or not she was diseased.

She was asked to sign a document (or make her mark) agreeing to the examination, and told that if she did not sign she would be taken before a magistrate who would, on the word of the police, certify that she was a prostitute and order the examination. Many women must have felt that they had no option but to sign, not realising that in doing so they were admitting to being prostitutes whether or not they were. If a woman were found to have a venereal disease, she could be sent to a 'lock hospital' for up to nine months. If she were free of disease she would be sent back on the streets and expected to report back for regular examinations. If she refused an examination, or failed to report back for one, she could be sent to prison for three months with hard labour.

The Contagious Diseases Acts outraged many women. They were seen to be unjust and one-sided as none of the soldiers and sailors who used the prostitutes were forced to undergo medical examinations. The Acts blamed women for the spread of disease and showed the Victorian double standards in action. While the sin of 'vice' was preached against in every pulpit, the Government was making sure that its soldiers and sailors had access to disease-free prostitutes. The findings of the Royal Commission that dealt with the objections to the Contagious Diseases Acts are held in the National Archives (WO 33/27). They give the official reason why men were not examined. They claim 'there is no comparison to be made between prostitutes and the men who consort with them. With the one sex the offence is committed as a matter of gain; with the other it is an irregular indulgence of a natural impulse'.

The most alarming aspect of the Contagious Diseases Acts was that a woman could be suspected of prostitution simply by being in the 'wrong part' of town. There were reports of at least one 'respectable' woman who was so ashamed at being mistaken for a prostitute and so humiliated by the forced examination, that she subsequently committed suicide. After a long and vigorous campaign, the Contagious Diseases Acts were repealed in 1886.

but to placate parents and to ensure that the girls did not lose their femininity they were also taught deportment, decorum and modesty. Emily Davies, an experienced campaigner on several women's issues, spent much of her time fighting for women's rights to higher education. She was one of the founders of Girton College, the first woman's college at Cambridge (see box, p. 106), and was one of those responsible for persuading London University to open their degrees to women.

In 1870 the Government made elementary education up to the age of 10 compulsory for all children. Although the Education Act included girls, little thought was given to their education. Much of their curriculum was devoted to subjects like laundry, housewifery and cooking, subjects that they could learn at home. Recognising this, the authorities often turned a blind eye to the frequent absences of girls kept at home to help mother. In schools in the poorer areas, several girls would be missing from class on a washday. Working class girls rarely went on to secondary education, as most ended up working in domestic service or in factories.

By the 1890s, it was becoming common for single, middle class women to go out to work. They were teachers in the new schools created by compulsory education; they found jobs in the large department stores that sprang up in the cities and large towns; and they were moving into offices to use the new typewriting machines. They were nurses and a few were doctors. Educated, single, and financially independent, they had opinions of their own and were prepared to voice them. Some rejected the elaborate clothing of the time and wore simpler and in some cases more 'mannish' clothes. Scathingly referred to as the 'new woman' they terrified the male establishment. They were pilloried in the press and portrayed as abnormal creatures whose very existence threatened, not only the fabric of society, but also the future of the British race.

By the time of Queen Victoria's death in 1901, although women were still second class citizens and still seen as being inferior to men, they had made some progress towards improving their status in society and in the home. In spite of the Queen's appeal in 1870 to 'everyone who can speak or write to join in checking this mad wicked folly of women's rights, with all its attendant horrors, on which her poor sex is bent', they had fought and won several campaigns. Many more of them were educated and many were critical of the status quo. They wanted change and they wanted a voice. Women had been campaigning for the vote since the 1860s. By the end of Victoria's reign, many 'new women' had lost patience with the old methods. They were ready to take the twentieth century by storm.

Deeds not words

How long you women have been trying for the vote. For my part, I mean to get it.

CHRISTABEL PANKHURST

The twentieth century opened with the death of Queen Victoria, the queen who, while happy to reign over a vast empire herself, held rigid and narrow views on a woman's place and how her fellow women should behave. Given how outraged she had been when Lady Amberley had spoken in favour of women's suffrage (see p.6), it is as well that she died when she did. For, within a few years of her death, women were not only using the peaceful, constitutional means she had considered so unladylike, they were going much further in their demand for the vote. Had she lived for another eight years she would have had to contend with the knowledge that Lady Constance Lytton (see profile, p.27), the daughter of one of her ladies-in-waiting, had been arrested and sent to prison for the cause.

By the start of the twentieth century, women, or at least some of them, had become seasoned campaigners. As well as their success in improving the rights of married women and their victory over the Contagious Diseases Acts, they had gained a foothold in local government. They were entitled to become poor law guardians, stand for election to school boards and, providing they met the property qualifications, allowed to vote in local government elections. Political parties were quick to capitalise on women's campaigning abilities. While they would not commit themselves to giving women the vote in general elections, they had allowed them to form separate associations such as the Conservative's Primrose League and the Women's Liberal Federation to help with the campaigns of male candidates.

Mrs Pankhurst and the Women's Social and Political Union

In October 1903, Mrs Pankhurst, frustrated by the lack of success in the long campaign to win the vote and mistrustful of the promises of politicians which came to nothing, formed the Women's Social and Political Union (WSPU) with the slogan 'Deeds not words'. Her daughters Christabel, Sylvia and Adela all joined her in the campaign. In her autobiography, *My Own Story*, she explained that she wanted 'women to demand immediate enfranchisement … through political action'. Like her daughter Christabel, she was determined to get the vote. Her experience as a poor law guardian and as a registrar of births and deaths had convinced her that the law would continue to treat women unfairly until they could vote in general elections.

By the time Mrs Pankhurst formed the WSPU, women had been campaigning for the vote for almost forty years. When they won the right to vote in local government elections in 1869, many of them must have believed that they would soon be able to vote in general elections. They were wrong. In spite of pledges of support from an increasing number of MPs and a number of private members' bills, women were no nearer to gaining the vote at the beginning of the twentieth century than they were at the start of the campaign.

By 1903, the suffragists' patient lobbying of Parliament and cultivation of sympathetic MPs was no longer considered shocking. Indeed, if Mrs Pankhurst is to be believed, it had become little more than a cosy ritual. In 1903 she joined women in a deputation to the House of Commons where they met friendly MPs to discuss the issue of women's suffrage. At the end of the meeting she made her presence felt by asking awkward questions. Making it clear that she was not interested in empty expressions of support, she wanted to know exactly what and when the MPs were going to do something about giving women the vote. Her

OPPOSITE
Annie Kenney (left) with Christabel Pankhurst. By the time this photograph was taken in 1906 they had already served a prison sentence in their fight for the vote.

direct questions embarrassed the MPs and irritated the other suffragists, who felt that her behaviour had ruined the good impression they had made.

When in 1904 yet another private member's bill in favour of women's suffrage was talked out (see box), Mrs Pankhurst committed the first act of militancy by protesting outside Parliament. From then on, convinced that women would only get the vote if it became government policy, she concentrated the efforts of the WSPU on putting pressure on the Government. History taught her that the nineteenth century suffrage reforms, which had given an increasing number of men the vote, had only been won after a great deal of political agitation. Men had demonstrated, rioted and resorted to arson during their long fight. At this stage, however, although she wanted more direct action, violence was the last thing on her mind.

Peaceful militancy

In the past, suffragists had campaigned for the vote by writing pamphlets, sending letters to influential men, organising petitions and persuading an MP to present a private member's bill. The whole emphasis of the traditional

Mrs Pankhurst in 1908. She was an eloquent and passionate speaker, and it was claimed that her voice was so clear and compelling that that she never needed a microphone – not even in a venue as large as the Albert Hall.

Private members' bills

Every MP has the right to present a bill to Parliament but it has to go through many stages and face many obstacles before it can become law. In 1904 a private member's bill in favour of women's suffrage was due for discussion after a roadways lighting bill. Much to Mrs Pankhurst's annoyance, MPs against women's suffrage deliberately kept discussing the lighting of carts until there was only half an hour of Parliamentary time left. Although the bill on women's suffrage was introduced there was no time to debate it and the measure was lost. Another way of killing a private member's bill was for the Government to refuse to give it enough time to become law. The Government did this on a number of occasions. A third way was for the Government to persuade MPs to vote against the bill, promising them a government-backed bill at some future date. As Mrs Pankhurst realised, the only sure way of getting a bill to become law was for it to have government support.

campaign was on converting individual MPs to the cause in the hope that they would eventually win over the majority. Although this was a good idea in theory, it did not work. There had been a majority in favour of women's suffrage in the House of Commons since the late nineteenth century but, for a variety of reasons, every private member's bill in favour of women's suffrage had failed to become law.

Realising the futility of the old methods, Mrs Pankhurst embarked on a strategy to change public opinion by holding meetings, distributing leaflets and by making women's suffrage an election issue. During the 1906 general election campaign she encouraged her supporters to bring up the topic at every opportunity. Once it became clear that the newly elected Liberal government had no intention of giving women the vote, Christabel made the decision to oppose all government candidates at by-elections, whether or not they supported women's suffrage. She believed that this, together with a change in public opinion, would be a better way to persuade the Government to change its mind. Several Liberals lost by-elections this way, including Winston Churchill who was then found a safe seat elsewhere.

The new methods certainly attracted publicity. In 1905 Christabel Pankhurst and Annie Kenney (see profile, p.20) attended a meeting held by two prominent Liberals and asked whether a Liberal government would give votes to women. At that time women were expected to remain silent during political meetings so the question was an act of militancy in itself. Their question was repeatedly ignored and they were ejected from the meeting even though men in the audience were free to ask questions. Before leaving the hall they unfurled a banner with their new slogan, 'Votes for women'. Outside they protested, were arrested and charged with obstruction. They received a fine, but although Mrs Pankhurst offered to pay it Christabel refused, and she and Annie Kenney became the first women to go to prison for the vote. Christabel's tactic paid off, as the following day the newspapers were full of the incident.

During 1906 several women were imprisoned for doing little more than attempting to lobby MPs and members of the Government. The *Daily Mail* coined the term 'suffragettes' to distinguish militants from the traditional suffragists. The suffragettes' new campaign inspired the traditional National Union of Women's Suffrage Societies (NUWSS) to become more pro-active. Suffragists held public meetings and campaigned on behalf of any candidate who promised to support women's suffrage. In February 1907, they went further and organised their first large demonstration, known as the 'Mud March' because of the muddy conditions in Hyde Park. As a result of the ensuing publicity, public support grew, more women joined suffrage societies, and new societies, both militant and non-militant, were formed.

Annie Kenney (1879–1953)

In 1905 Annie Kenney (see photograph, p.16), a mill girl and trade unionist from Lancashire, went to a talk given by Christabel Pankhurst. That simple decision affected the rest of her life. Born in 1879, one of 11 children of working class parents, and forced through poverty to work in a factory from the age of 10, she nevertheless was brought up in a family where education and culture were important. As a result of meeting Christabel, she became part of the leadership of the suffragette movement, the only working class woman to achieve that status. Her sisters Jessie, Jenny and Nell also became suffragettes.

Within months of attending her first suffrage meeting, she and Christabel were serving the first prison sentences of the suffrage campaign. In 1906, she went to London to organise the campaign there. In June she was arrested when heading a deputation to Asquith's home and served another prison sentence, this time of six weeks. She was arrested again in October 1906 for taking part in a demonstration in the House of Commons and was sent to prison for another two months. Over the course of the militant campaign she served several prison sentences and underwent both hunger, and hunger and thirst, strikes.

In 1907 she became a paid organiser for the WSPU. When the leaders of the WSPU were arrested in 1912, Christabel escaped to Paris and left her in control. Each weekend, Annie travelled to Paris for a meeting with Christabel. In 1913 she was tried and sentenced to three years in prison. Although she went on hunger, and hunger and thirst, strikes she was never forcibly fed. A file in the National Archives (HO 45/10700) shows that on one occasion she was not released under the 'Cat and Mouse Act' until she was 'in a state of collapse'. The file also contains details of her failed appeal to the Archbishop of Canterbury for sanctuary. On 28 May 1914 she was given another temporary discharge and, as usual, failed to return on the set date; this time, however, she successfully evaded the police and was never rearrested.

In 1907 the WSPU held the first of several 'Women's Parliaments' at Caxton Hall which met the day after the official opening of Parliament. When it became clear that the Government had no plans to deal with women's suffrage, a series of deputations was sent out to the House of Commons. A wall of police met the peaceful procession of women and mounted police charged at them. Although people had a right to petition Parliament, the suffragettes were effectively denied this right and police were used to prevent them reaching the House of Commons. It was a scene to be repeated time and again, with increasing violence, over the next seven years. Dozens of women were arrested as they tried to get through the police lines. They were charged with obstruction or with resisting the police and, when they refused to pay their fines, were sent to jail.

In 1908, in response to anti-suffragist claims that only a few women wanted the vote, the WSPU organised a mass demonstration. Three days before the event, they hired a steam launch and sailed it from Battersea to the House of Commons. The timing, according to *The Times*, was perfect. When the boat reached Westminster, approximately 800 people were taking tea on the terrace of the House of Commons. Their attention was drawn to the launch by the sound of a brass band and the waving suffragettes. Banners announced the demonstration and one stated 'Cabinet ministers especially welcome'. The next day the newspapers reported the incident, giving the demonstration maximum publicity.

As a result of that publicity, the demonstration on 21 June was hugely successful. Thousands of women dressed in white and wearing sashes in the WSPU colours (see box) marched to Hyde Park where between a quarter and half a million people, estimates vary, gathered for the demonstration. There were twenty platforms for the many speakers, who came from all walks of life. Given that only a minority of those who agree with a cause attend demonstrations, the Government had been given an answer to the question of whether or not women wanted the vote. The demonstration had absolutely no effect on Asquith, the Prime Minister.

Asquith's repeated refusal to meet suffragette deputations or to accept their petitions drove them to devise ingenious attempts to reach him. On 17 January 1908, three women went to Downing Street to put their views to the Cabinet. They were pushed away by police but one managed to get inside. While the police were distracted, two others chained themselves to the railings and made a speech calling for votes for women. Others followed suit. In October of that year, Muriel Matters and Helen Fox chained themselves to the grille of the Ladies' Gallery in the House of Commons. The chains had two purposes: they gave the suffragettes time to make a speech before they were cut free and, more importantly, they were a powerful symbol of women's lack of freedom.

These and similar actions kept the issue of women's suffrage in the news. In February 1909, Muriel Matters pulled another headline-grabbing stunt when she dropped fifty-six pounds of leaflets across London from a small airship. A week later, two suffragettes, Miss McLellan and Miss Solomon, posted themselves to the Prime Minister as human letters. Only the messenger was allowed in and the 'letters' were rejected in spite having been paid for. In December 1909, Jessica

A riot of colour

The many suffrage processions and demonstrations provided the crowds with a spectacular sight. The different suffrage societies designed banners, rosettes and sashes in their own colours. The WSPU chose purple for justice, white for purity, and green for hope as their colours, and their members were encouraged to wear a uniform of white jacket with a green or purple skirt and a coloured hat. Several societies chose green as one of their colours including: The Actresses' Franchise League – pink and green; the Women's Freedom League – green, white and gold; and the National Union of Women's Suffrage Societies – red, white and green. Writers chose black, white and gold and artists blue, black and yellow.

VOTES FOR WOMEN
DEPUTATION
WILL WAIT ON YOU AT THE
HOUSE OF
COMMONS
WEDNESDAY
AT 4 PM.

TO THE RIGHT HON.
H. H.
ASQUITH
10, DOWNING STREET.
S.W.

Miss Daisy Solomon (on the right) and Miss McLellan, accompanied by a telegraph messenger, on their way to Downing Streeet, having 'posted' themselves to the Prime Minister in an attempt to get him to listen to them. Asquith refused to see them but it proved to be a good publicity stunt and was widely reported.

Kenney, one of Annie's sisters, tried, and failed, to see Asquith by disguising herself as a telegraph boy.

Anti-suffragists

Queen Victoria might have died in 1901, but many of the ideas current at the start of her reign lived on well into the twentieth century. Even though women had been actively involved in local politics for decades, some still argued that politics was a man's world and that it was against the laws of nature for women to govern (they conveniently forgot that Queen Victoria had reigned for more than sixty years). They also disregarded women's work in local government, claiming that, as local politics dealt with domestic issues such as education and poverty, it was well within a woman's sphere.

Whatever the reason given, fear seems to be at the root of the anti-suffragist opposition. Some feared that women would lose their femininity once they could vote, while others worried that the relationship between husband and wife would suffer. Presumably they thought that having gained the vote women would demand to be consulted on decision-making at home. Some men were anxious about the consequences of giving women the vote as they outnumbered men in the population. Others were concerned that women's more passive natures would lead them to vote against the use of force in international disputes. Linked to this was the belief that if Britain gave women the vote the country would lose respect in the Empire. Once again they seem to have ignored the fact of Queen Victoria's reign.

The 'antis' attacked the suffragettes in a number of ways but a favourite tactic was to imply that the only women who wanted the vote were frustrated spinsters. The ugly spinster who could not get a man was a favourite of cartoonists. They also accused the suffragettes of being man haters, ignoring the fact that many were married. It was a measure of the inadequacy of their arguments that they had to resort to such crude attacks.

The anti-suffragist novelist, Marie Corelli, who is quoted in *The Virago Book of Suffragettes*, held some incredible views. She claimed that women already had all the power they needed through their femininity. She accused suffragettes of wanting women to exchange their 'birthright of simple womanliness for a political mess of pottage'. Instead she recommended that women sat at home and spun a pretty web that men would fall into and become their prisoners. She had the grace to accept that some men mistreated women but then blamed this on their mothers for failing to bring them up properly. While her attack on women's suffrage cannot have been taken seriously, her views would have provided fuel for those who argued that women were too silly to be given the vote.

Another controversial view came from Asquith, the suffragettes' most powerful opponent. According to a letter from George Bernard Shaw to *The Times*, quoted in *The Virago Book of Suffragettes*, Asquith argued against giving women the vote 'on the ground that woman is not the female of the human species but a distinct and inferior species'. Asquith also said that a woman was no more qualified to vote than a rabbit. His view that women were not fully human goes a long way to explain why the suffragettes were so harshly treated both when sentenced and when they were imprisoned. It also goes some way to explain why, in spite of growing support for women's suffrage both in the country and in Parliament, private members' bills to give women the vote repeatedly failed to become law.

Although the anti-suffragists, both male and female, argued that women belonged in separate spheres, they did not seem to see anything contradictory in encouraging women to campaign against the vote. In 1908, when it seemed that the case for women's suffrage was making some progress, they went further and formed the Women's National Anti-Suffrage League. It is ironic that, through involving women in the campaign against the vote, anti-suffragists were proving that women were perfectly capable of being involved in national politics.

The census boycott of 1911

Asquith had often argued that few women wanted the vote. The census provided women with another chance to prove him wrong. When the Women's Freedom League called for a boycott of the 1911 census it was supported by the other suffrage societies, both militant and non-militant. As a passive form of resistance it appealed to large numbers of women across the country: with the rallying cry of 'No vote – no census', women of all classes defied the Government and refused to be counted. Many of them evaded the census by staying away from home on census night. A few did this by hiring gypsy caravans and spending the night out on the moors. Emily Davison, who was later killed at the Derby (see p. 33), spent the night in the crypt of the House of Commons and was found the next morning close to a sign stating 'Guy Fawkes was killed here'.

To make it easier for women to spend the night away from home in safety, all-night events and 'at homes' were held across the country. In London special events were organised with concerts in the Queen's Hall and the Scala Theatre. At midnight women gathered in Trafalgar Square and walked around to attract attention to the boycott before going to the Aldwych skating rink where many of them spent the night. While some skated, others enjoyed the entertainment provided by supporters from the Actresses' Franchise League. Refreshments from a nearby all-night café kept them going until the morning.

Women householders who were prepared to pay fines resisted the census by refusing to complete their forms. One woman, who must have had in mind a Law Lords' decision of 1908 which stated that the term 'persons' didn't include women, carefully entered details of her manservant and added that, although there were many women in the house, there were no other persons. In some cases, sympathetic male householders refused to enter the names of any women in their homes and added a note explaining what they had done. Many women went further and opened their homes to census evaders. Some simply provided a place to sleep while others, partly to fit more women into their homes, organised all-night parties.

Some non-householders, wanting to take a more active role, rented empty properties for census night. They filled these with dozens of women and returned their forms with the slogan 'No vote – no census'. These women had no intention of paying fines and were prepared to go to prison. The number of women that could be put up by a householder ranged from a few to more than 100. According to Mrs Pankhurst, 16 wealthy women in Birmingham packed their homes with census evaders and, elsewhere, a head of a college opened her doors to more than 300 women.

Although failure to complete a census form carried the heavy penalty of a £5 fine, or a month's imprisonment, the Government decided not to prosecute, claiming the effect on the census was insignificant. Its leniency, however, is suspect. Had the boycott been limited to the actions of a few militants then, going by the Government's record, the resisters would have been severely punished. It is far more likely that, faced with the huge publicity that would be generated by thousands of court cases across the country, it chose to play down the whole affair.

Prison and prisoners

Between 1905 and 1914 more than 1,000 suffragettes were sent to prison and many served more than one prison sentence. Although they claimed they were political prisoners and should be sentenced as such, magistrates, acting under government instructions, treated them as common criminals. This distinction made a huge difference to the way they were treated. Political prisoners were sentenced to the first division and had many privileges not available to common criminals. The only real hardship was their loss of liberty; political prisoners did not have to work, they could wear their own clothes and they could rent a furnished cell if they chose. They were also allowed to have magazines and books from outside and could buy in food and wine. Once a fortnight they were allowed a visitor and could send and receive one letter.

Common criminals, however, were put in either the second or third division. There was little difference between the two except that the second division was usually reserved for the more 'respectable' criminal. Middle class offenders were likely to be put there away from the 'rougher', working class criminals in the third division. In sharp contrast to the treatment of political prisoners, criminals were kept in solitary confinement for the first four weeks

The WSPU periodical, Votes for Women, revealed the barbaric treatment of suffragettes by the prison authorities. The Home Office kept a close eye on the militant societies and they filed this issue on 3 January 1910.

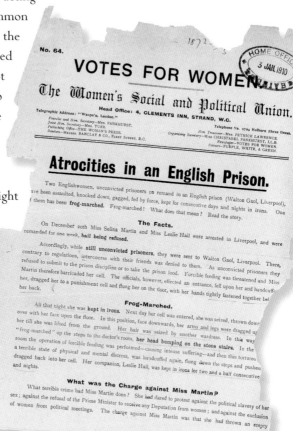

and only allowed out of their cells for one hour a day. The cells were airless and barely furnished. They had to wear prison clothes and eat prison food. All second and third division prisoners had to work, either cleaning, knitting, sewing or darning socks. Some were sentenced to hard labour.

Suffragettes objected to being treated as common criminals and most protested against their sentences. A file in the National Archives (HO 144/1047) contains a petition from Alison Neilans who was sent to prison for three months for 'interfering' with ballot papers. She argued that when she poured a liquid into a ballot box she was not committing electoral fraud but making a political protest and so belonged in the first division as a political prisoner. She compared her case with that of a man whose actions had 'caused the death of men, women and children', yet was still treated as a political prisoner. In spite of her valid argument, her request was ignored. She subsequently went on hunger strike in protest and was forcibly fed.

Although the Government insisted that the decision where to place a prisoner rested with the magistrates, it could and did intervene when it chose. A file in the National Archives (HO 144/891) deals with objections to the harsh sentences meted out in 1908 by Mr Hopkins, a magistrate who did not accept that suffragettes had a serious motive for their actions. He seemed to believe that their protests were for 'show' and, to teach them a lesson, he sentenced them to the third division. Mary Manning was among those sentenced to a month's imprisonment in the third division for 'wilfully obstructing a policeman' even though it was her first offence.

Her father, whose letter is in the file, wrote to the Home Secretary, Herbert Gladstone, requesting a modification in her sentence. He was clearly anxious to prevent his daughter, whom he described as 'a clergyman's daughter, a graduate in honours of London University' from having to mix with 'drunks, thieves and rogues' in the third division. The Home Office wrote to the magistrate to remind him that 'these prisoners whose antecedents are respectable and their general character good appear to belong to the class for whom the Second Division was intended by Parliament'. He was also told that Gladstone did not accept that suffragettes were political prisoners but stressed that they belonged in the second division because of their social class.

The harsh sentences meted out to suffragettes in the early days brought them a great deal of sympathy. In October 1908, when Mrs Pankhurst and others were taken to Bow Street police station too late to be granted bail, they were expected to spend the night in cells with no beds in them. As soon as he heard of the situation, James Murray, MP for East Aberdeenshire, came to their aid and arranged for beds and food to be brought from the Savoy Hotel. The sympathetic

Lady Constance Lytton alias 'Jane Wharton' (1869-1923)

Lady Constance Lytton is best known for the way she disguised herself as a working class woman in order to expose the Government's preferential treatment of the well-connected suffragettes. There was no suffragette with more powerful connections than hers. Born in 1869, she was the daughter of the first Earl of Lytton, Viceroy of India. Her mother had been a lady-in-waiting to Queen Victoria, and her brother, Lord Lytton, a supporter of women's suffrage, sat in the House of Lords.

Although she had a heart condition, and could have been excused from undertaking prison sentences, she went to prison on four occasions. The first was in 1909 when she was sent to Holloway for her part in a deputation. Once there she was sent to the hospital ward. In spite of her objections, she was not removed to a cell until she began to scratch 'Votes for women' across her chest in protest. She served her second imprisonment in Newcastle Prison where, having started a hunger strike, she was released after only two days because of her heart condition.

In 1910, ashamed of being given preferential treatment, she rejoined the WSPU as 'Jane Wharton' and disguised herself as a poor seamstress. Having noticed that less attractive women were treated more harshly, she made herself as ugly as possible. She did the job so well that she wondered 'is the Punch version of the suffragette overdone?' As Jane Wharton, she was sentenced to 14 days' imprisonment with hard labour in the third division. She went on hunger strike and was forcibly fed eight times without any medical examination.

When rumours of her real identity reached the prison authorities they released her on the grounds of her weight loss. Records in the National Archives (HO 144/1054/187986) show that on 19 January 1910 a medical report stated 'nothing to report today doing well'. The following day the report stated 'bears artificial feeding badly', yet they continued to force feed her. On the 21 January the comment was 'not strong fairly cheerful', yet on 22 January the report stated 'recommend for release at once'. Although the authorities denied knowing who she was, on 23 January they released her into the care of her sister.

The WSPU took full advantage of the situation and prepared a leaflet for distribution at polling stations during the general election. A copy of the leaflet, which is in the file mentioned above, was sent to the Home Secretary together with a letter from a man who described himself as 'formerly a staunch Liberal'. The man, whose signature is illegible, added that he had voted Conservative as he objected to 'the torture of political offenders by forcible feeding, especially when discrimination is made between persons of rank on the one hand, and working people on the other'. Lady Constance had made her point but at a cost. As a result of her forcible feeding her mild heart condition deteriorated into a serious one.

It took many months for her to recover from her ordeal and in the autumn of the same year she suffered what she described as 'a slight heart seizure'. Once she had recovered she continued to work for the cause and in November 1911 was imprisoned for the fourth time. She chose prison in spite of having had a series of heart seizures after making speeches and 'heart collapse' after her arrest. A stroke in 1912, which left her partly paralysed, stopped her from taking part in further militancy but, with her left hand, she wrote letters and pamphlets and her book Prisons and Prisoners. She died in 1923.

hotel management did more than was asked. They also sent three waiters to serve the food, complete with flowers, silver cutlery and candlesticks. The police must have been amazed to see such a banquet served within the confines of their station.

It is a measure of their commitment that so many suffragettes, especially those from comfortable backgrounds, should have braved prison not just once but, knowing how bad the conditions were, returned again and again in their determination to win the vote. When Mrs Pethwick-Lawrence, one of the suffragette leaders, first went to Holloway, the shock of the dirt, the lack of air and the evil smells gave her a nervous breakdown and she was moved to the prison hospital. She was released soon after and went abroad to recuperate. In spite of this she not only endured another two prison sentences, but went on hunger strike and was forcibly fed.

In her book *Prisons and Prisoners*, Lady Constance Lytton describes the awful conditions. She was particularly revolted by prison clothing, especially the 'duster', a piece of cloth which was used either as a handkerchief or worn as a neckerchief – there was no way of knowing how the previous user had used it. As she described items of clothing as coming from the laundry 'with many stains ... looking in many respects as if they had not been washed', her revulsion is understandable. It is interesting that, as a result of the many suffragette complaints, conditions in Holloway were improved.

Hunger strikes

In July 1909, Marion Wallace Dunlop went on hunger strike in protest against being refused political prisoner status and was released after 91 hours without food. Others followed her example and they too were released after several days on hunger strike. Although a few people felt that the suffragettes should be allowed to die, the Government was anxious not to create any martyrs. Whenever hunger strikers were released they were met by a welcoming party and looked after by friends until they recovered.

After a number of suffragettes had been released in this way King Edward VII intervened. On 13 August 1909, he sent a letter to Herbert Gladstone, the Home Secretary, asking why women were being released from prison when there were methods for dealing with the situation. Gladstone took the hint and in September forcible feeding of the hunger strikers began. The decision caused a public outcry and sympathetic MPs repeatedly brought the matter up in the Commons. It was harsh treatment indeed. For although a few of the suffragettes were in prison for stone throwing, the majority were jailed for doing no more than pushing past

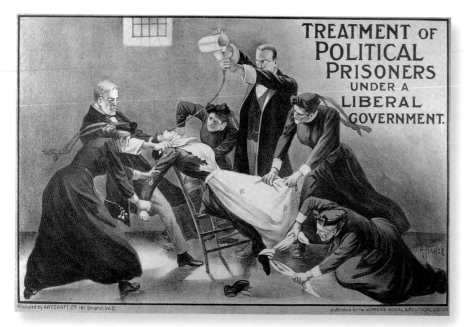

TREATMENT OF POLITICAL PRISONERS UNDER A LIBERAL GOVERNMENT.

Produced by ARTCRAFT L^{td} 161 Strand. W.C.

published by the WOMEN'S SOCIAL & POLITICAL UNION

Posters like this one created for the WSPU in 1910 brought the horrors of forcible feeding to the attention of the public. It is a measure of the determination and strength of feeling of the hunger-strikers that they were prepared to endure such torture, time and again.

policemen who were preventing them from taking a deputation to the Prime Minister, something that they had a legal right to do.

Forcible feeding was not only extremely painful and unpleasant, it could be dangerous. Suffragettes were fed by passing a tube into the stomach by way of the nose or the mouth. A wooden or steel gag was used to force and keep their mouths open, and wardresses held them down while food was poured into them. Gums were cut and teeth and crowns were often broken in the process, as a letter from Lady Lytton's dentist, which she quotes in her book, confirmed. In October 1909 116 doctors signed a 'memorial' against forcible feeding, claiming that it was a dangerous procedure and that accidents were likely to happen. They were to be proved right. In 1913, in the struggle to feed Lillian Lenton, doctors poured food into her lungs.

In protest against being forcibly fed, Emily Davison barricaded herself in her cell only for the authorities to aim a fire hose at her before breaking down the cell door. She later won damages for this treatment but the judge in the case was not sympathetic and she received a fraction of the £100 she had claimed. She continued to protest at every opportunity. A file in the National Archives (PCOM 8/174) shows that on another occasion she threw herself over the prison staircase but, in spite of being bruised and shaken, she was deemed fit enough to be fed through a nasal tube.

Apart from the brutality of forcible feeding, a worrying aspect of the process was the lack of hygiene practised in the prisons. The tubes used were not kept in hygienic conditions nor, it seemed, were they ever disinfected. Doctors also showed a total lack of sensitivity towards the prisoners: vegetarians and teetotallers were fed beef tea and brandy.

The treatment of the hunger strikers infuriated the suffragettes and some responded with increased violence. In the House of Commons, George Lansbury accused Asquith of torturing women. He was not alone in this belief and the public outcry was strong. In an attempt to avert the bad publicity and the daily questions in the House of Commons, the Government passed The Prisoner's (Temporary Discharge for Ill-Health) Act in 1913. This soon became known as the 'Cat and Mouse Act'. It provided for hunger strikers to be released on licence once they became too weak to remain in prison. They were expected to return when they had recovered. Many went into hiding but they were usually rearrested. Suffragettes who were released in this way became known as 'mice' and the house where many of them went to recuperate was known as Mouse Castle.

Violence at the deputation of 18 November 1910, known as 'Black Friday'. Most of the photographs showing police brutality were suppressed while others which showed suffragettes behaving aggressively were freely published.

Escalating violence

The suffragettes are often associated with violence but, for the first few years of the militant campaign, the violence came from their opponents. *The Virago Book of Suffragettes* includes a piece by Margaret Nevinson describing some of the violent

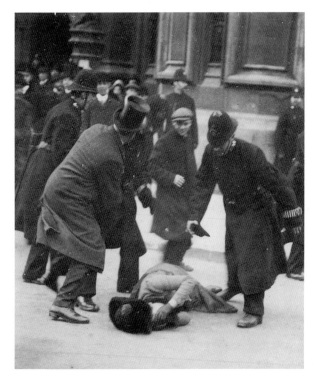

behaviour that she and other suffragettes encountered whenever they held public meetings. She particularly disliked speaking on street corners and in the open because of the 'rotten eggs and garbage' that was thrown at them. Sometimes they also had to contend with cayenne pepper blown at them from bellows and, on at least one occasion, rats were released into the audience of a Women's Freedom League meeting.

Although Margaret Nevinson wrote that on occasions the police came to their rescue when hostile crowds were too threatening, many suffragettes, especially those who went on deputations to the House of Commons, saw a more brutal side to the police. In her book, Lady Constance Lytton describes how she was thrown about by policemen when she went on such a deputation. The worst of the violence towards the suffragettes, however, occurred on 18 November

1910, a day remembered as Black Friday. A file in the National Archives (MEPO 3/203) contains details of the incident. Documents in the file make disturbing reading for they show that women were badly beaten, insulted and sexually assaulted by the police. A memorandum to the Home Office, which accompanied a request for a public inquiry, suggests that the police believed their duty was to terrorise the women as well as prevent them from reaching the House of Commons.

The memorandum includes material from doctors and eye-witnesses as well as from the women involved. A man who rescued Henria Williams from a policeman later described her as being in a 'semi-fainting condition, so much so that she could hardly stand'. He also referred to the 'entirely unnecessary violence and brutality of the police'. On 1 January 1911, six weeks after her brutal treatment, Henria died of heart failure. Several other women were seriously injured and never fully recovered from their ordeal. Mary Clarke, Mrs Pankhurst's sister, was badly treated on Black Friday. A few days later she broke a window in protest and was sent to prison for one month. She was released on 21 December and died a few days later on Christmas Day.

The police were also accused of indecently assaulting women. There were claims that some groped women's breasts or put their hands under their skirts. Such treatment would be bad enough in the twenty-first century but in 1910 it caused the women terrible shame, and was resented far more than the physical beatings. One young girl was labelled a prostitute and forced to walk several yards with police holding her skirts over her head. In another case, a man in the crowd indecently assaulted a woman while a policeman held her hands behind her back. The policeman made no attempt to protect her, possibly because many of the 'roughs' in the crowd were plain-clothes policemen.

Although there had been isolated cases of stone throwing, the militant campaign did not become violent until 1909. Initially the violence was mild and took the form of window breaking, first in Downing Street and government offices in Whitehall. For some, stone throwing was a way of ensuring a quick arrest and of avoiding the prolonged rough handling by crowds and the police. As frustrations with the Government grew, stone throwing spread, and in the lead up to the 1910 general election suffragettes, banned from Liberal meetings, took every opportunity to harass Liberals, especially Cabinet Ministers and the Prime Minister.

While many denounced this increased militancy, some anti-suffragists inadvertently incited them to further violence. One was Mr Hobhouse MP who, in denying that women wanted the vote, compared them with the men who burned Nottingham Castle in their agitation for male suffrage. He was not the first nor the

LILLIAN FORRE

only man to take this stance. Lloyd George made similar comments condoning the destruction of property in the case of oppressed men without democratic rights. Suffragettes rewarded him for this speech by blowing up his newly built house.

Although the suffragettes called a truce in February 1910 while sympathetic MPs worked hard to get a suffrage bill through Parliament, violence erupted again in 1911 when Asquith torpedoed the bill. Emily Davison set fire to a letterbox and mass window smashing raids took place in London in 1911 and 1912. Once Mrs Pankhurst urged her supporters to rebellion the violence became more serious. As well as firing letterboxes, suffragettes destroyed golf greens and cut telegraph wires. In 1913 violence escalated still further and a few suffragettes, accepting what they saw as the incitement of Hobhouse and Lloyd George, set fire to and blew up empty properties. Although this level of violence lost them the support of even militant suffragettes, by now both Mrs Pankhurst and Christabel believed that the only way to gain the vote was to show the Government that women were ungovernable without it.

The most shocking event in 1913 took place on 4 June, when race-goers at the Derby saw Emily Davison rush out onto the course at Tattenham corner and grab the reins of Anmer, the King's horse. She was trampled by the horse and later died of her injuries. Mrs Pankhurst made much of the fact that the only deaths and injuries that resulted from militancy had been to suffragettes themselves. She had made it clear, when calling women to rebellion, that they had to stop short of injury to others. However it is not difficult to imagine that had she died as a result of her hunger and thirst strikes (and on one occasion she was a whisper away from death before she was released), her more radical followers would have ignored her plea and avenged her death. That possibility, however, was averted by the outbreak of the First World War.

OPPOSITE
These photographs taken from a police file of known militant suffragettes in 1914 give some indication of the different ages and classes of women involved in the movement. Not all would have been correctly identified as many of them used a number of aliases. Police photographs of suffragettes thought to be 'dangerous' to works of art were shared with other police forces and sent to art galleries and museums.

1 Margaret Scott, 2 Olive Hoskin, 3 Margaret McFarlane, 4 Mary Wyan, alias Hallie Taylor, 5 Annie Bell, alias Hannah Booth, alias Elizabeth Ball, 6 Jane Short, alias Rachel Peace, 7 Gertrude Mary Ansell, 8 Maud Brindley, 9 Verity Oates, 10 Evelyn Manesta, 11 Mary Richardson, 12 May Dennis, alias Lilian Lenton, 13 Kitty Marion, 14 Lillian Forrester, 15 Miss Johansen, 16 Clara Giveen, 17 Jennie Baines, 18 Miriam Pratt.

On her their lives depend

In mould the rose unfolds. The soul through blood and tears.

MEREDITH, QUOTED BY VERA BRITTAIN IN HER DIARIES

When war was declared on 4 August 1914, no one could have predicted the effect it was to have on women's lives. Had it been 'all over by Christmas', as so many believed, there would have been no appeals for women to come to the aid of their country. There would have been no calls for munitions workers, no pleas for women to join the Land Army and no women's military services. Before the outbreak of war, some anti-suffragists had felt that giving women the vote would put the country's security at risk. They mistakenly believed that women were natural pacifists who would always vote against war, making the country seem weak to its enemies. When war did break out their fears proved to be unfounded as the large number of patriotic women anxious to make a contribution to the war effort far outweighed the number of women pacifists.

The suffragette reaction

Within days of the declaration of war, Mrs Pankhurst declared a truce until it was over. She was fiercely patriotic, believing that the country's need took priority over the suffrage issue. As far as she was concerned, there was no point in having the vote without a country to vote in. The Government declared an amnesty and imprisoned suffragettes were released. Christabel returned from exile in Paris to join her mother in her support of the war, and proceeded to make speeches attacking the 'German peril'. Sylvia Pankhurst, however, was a pacifist, and much to her mother's dismay campaigned against the war while continuing her work with the women and poor in the East End of London.

Having called off all militant action, Mrs Pankhurst turned her attention to the war effort. Although she was in a weakened state, due to the countless hunger strikes she'd endured, her energy was undiminished and she was not about to use the ending of militancy as an excuse to take a rest from campaigning. Instead, in her own inimitable fashion, she threw herself into rousing women to join the war effort. When she discovered that some trade unions were making it difficult for women to contribute to the war effort by refusing to accept them in men's jobs, she began a vigorous campaign for the 'right to serve'.

Almost a year later, on 24 June 1915, she was still arguing for the 'right to serve'. In a speech made at the London Polytechnic she insisted that women should be utilised in the war effort. Her speech was reported in *The Times*. The following day, Lloyd George, who was then Munitions Minister, received a letter from Buckingham Palace with a suggestion from the King that Mrs Pankhurst could be made use of. It seems ironic that the Government, which had regarded her as an enemy of the state and imprisoned her on several occasions, should have been so keen on recruiting her help.

Within three weeks of the King's suggestion to Lloyd George and with the help of government funds, Mrs Pankhurst had organised a rally. On 17 July 1915, a great procession of approximately 30,000 women marched through London for 'the right to serve'. This was just the start of her activities and throughout the period she travelled around the country urging men and women to work hard for the war effort. She travelled as far as America and Russia drumming up support for the war. A less savoury element of her effort was to encourage her supporters to give a white feather, denoting cowardice, to any young man who was not in uniform. Young men, sometimes too young to enlist, were 'persuaded' to join up in this way.

The other suffrage societies also turned their efforts towards the war effort and, though they continued to discuss the vote with the Government, they called

OPPOSITE
This poster (c.1915) calling on women to enrol for work in the munitions factories was just one of a number designed to encourage them to volunteer for war work.

a halt to active campaigning. Although many suffragists, Mrs Fawcett among them, had argued in favour of a peaceful solution to the crisis in Europe, once war had been declared the majority dropped their pacifist stance fearing it would harm their cause.

Mrs Fawcett appealed to her members to join the war effort as a means of proving themselves worthy of the vote. In the suffrage magazine, *The Common Cause*, she wrote, 'Let us show ourselves worthy of citizenship, whether our claim to it be recognised or not'. When pacifists decided to attend the women's peace congress in the Hague in 1915 she refused to allow them to go as representatives of the National Union of Women's Suffrage Societies (NUWSS). Her main concern at all times was to keep women's suffrage a separate issue for fear of weakening it. She realised that any link between the suffrage campaign and pacifism would play into the hands of the anti-suffragists and would give them reason to accuse women of being unfit for citizenship.

Women's war work

At the very start of the war, women were not only having their offers to help with the war effort rejected, but many found themselves unemployed. As people started to economise, trade suffered and jobs were lost, especially in the textile mills in the north. Queen Mary was concerned enough to set up the Queen's 'Work for women fund'. The intention was to create workshops for unemployed women who would otherwise be forced to seek relief. Sylvia Pankhurst was so disgusted at the low level of wages being paid under the scheme that she referred to them as 'Queen Mary's sweatshops'.

Not all women faced unemployment. In the early months of the war, some were taking on jobs left vacant by a husband or brother who had joined up. Wives and sisters delivered milk, swept chimneys, cleaned windows and did similar types of work. This arrangement would have been regarded as a temporary measure as most people believed that the war would be over in a very short time. It ensured that the job was done, the family had an income and the man's job was protected.

Although the need to employ women did not arise during the first few months of the war, there was no objection to them doing charitable work. On 30 December 1914, under the headline 'A record of quiet service', *The Times* reported on the good work done by women workers of the Soldiers' and Sailors' Families' Association in helping servicemen's families made temporarily destitute by delays in paying the separation allowances they got while their husbands were serving away from home. Referring to 'duties which can best be performed by women', it also praised the women who met and cared for the refugees arriving from the continent.

Rent strikes

Patriotism during the war did not inspire everyone to work in harmony whatever the situation. In some areas women objected strongly to the conditions they found themselves in. Rent strikes broke out in Glasgow in 1915. The problem was triggered in June with the attempted eviction of a soldier's family. A crowd of angry neighbours, most of them women, intervened to prevent the eviction. Following this incident, a group of women organised a rent strike and refused to pay the increased rents. They set up mass pickets and bombarded anyone attempting to collect rents with flour, rotten fish and whatever else came to hand. In Glasgow the rent strikers had the support of workers in the shipyards and munitions, key industries during the war. As the strike spread to other areas the Government became concerned that essential production would be affected and later in 1915 they responded by passing a Rent Restriction Act.

By the beginning of 1915, however, the situation changed as it became clear that the war was going to last longer than predicted. The Government needed to act. It needed men for the front and it needed to increase armament production. The problem was that as more men joined up, the munitions factories were losing vital workers. As the 'right to serve' campaign showed, the simple solution was to employ women. In March 1915, the Board of Trade ordered a national register of women prepared to volunteer for war work and set up recruiting stations around the country where women could sign on. Within a few weeks more than 30,000 had answered the call but, although the women were willing, employers and unions still had to be convinced.

Women cleaning railway carriages. Even work like this was resented by a number of men who were worried that they would become unemployed after the war. It was a genuine fear as employers paid female staff a fraction of what men earned.

Some trade unions, especially in traditional male areas like heavy engineering, were strongly against women taking over men's jobs. Their main concern was to protect the jobs and rates of pay of their members and they feared that once employers had accepted women in the place of men they would continue to use them as a source of cheap labour. As women earned on average half the wage of a man the unions had a valid point. Unions also resisted the training of women for skilled jobs for the same reason. They finally relented after skilled jobs were divided so they became classed as semi-skilled, and after promises from the Government that women would be employed only for the duration of the war.

In spite of initial resistance, women soon found their way into all walks of life. In some cases they replaced men in jobs where women had already been accepted, such as clerical work and work as shop assistants. Newspapers encouraged women to contribute to the war effort by printing reports of their achievements and by praising them for their sterling work. The tone of some of the reports, especially in the early years of the war, is part patronising and part marvelling. It is as though the writers could hardly believe what they were reporting.

In a report headed 'New professions for women' dated 8 March 1915, *The Times* commented on work that women were doing in the railways. They reported that women were now employed in the accountancy and clerical departments, but had not yet been allowed to work in the booking offices, though they implied that this might come in time. When they reported that in Scotland women were employed as carriage cleaners they added that they had 'given every satisfaction', as though the fact that women were able to clean a railway carriage was something remarkable.

Two interesting snippets emerged from the same article. The first was that even though many women were employed as drivers, the authorities refused to license women who wanted to be taxi drivers. The second was a report of the creation of a new toy-making factory by the Women's Emergency Corps where the girls could earn up to £1 a week. To be reminded of toys amongst all the talk of war would have provided readers with a little light relief.

At first the sight of women doing what was traditionally a man's job sent shock waves through parts of the community, as an extract in *The Virago Book of Women and the Great War*, edited by Joyce Marlow, shows. When Margaret Cardell first drove a butcher's cart accompanied by the man she was to replace, she felt that everyone was staring at her. Once she had been trained and started delivering meat on her own, the reaction she met ranged from shock to hostility. One of her elderly male customers refused to speak to her and left his order on notes, which he would leave in different parts of his garden. It was some time before he would bring himself to speak to her.

Women working in a munitions factory – note that the supervisors are male. Although it was relatively well paid, this was dangerous work, but many preferred it to a life in domestic service.

Although women were doing men's work only a tiny minority ever received a man's wage and most received a lot less. During the First World War the demand for equal pay for equal work became a major issue for the first time. In Newcastle when women were refused a 5s. (25p) bonus paid to male tram-workers they went on strike. The strike was successful, as there were fears that it would spread to munitions workers. The women received the bonus but made no progress towards equal pay.

Women in munitions work were better paid than those in most other jobs, but their work was both unpleasant and dangerous. They worked with high explosives, and accidents in which women were killed and injured were not uncommon. Another danger came from handling and inhaling the chemicals. Girls who worked with TNT were known as 'canaries' because the chemicals turned their skin yellow and their hair a yellow or copper colour. The authorities played down the risks of working in munitions and patriotic propaganda played down the dangers to health, suggesting they were trivial when compared with what men faced at the front.

The Virago Book of Women and the Great War includes a report from *The Star* dated 7 December 1916, on an inquest on a girl of 16 who had died from TNT poisoning. According to a Dr Legge, TNT was only dangerous to those under the age of 18. The employer claimed that the girl had lied about her age and insisted that he only employed people between 18 and 45 years of age. He also said that, although he employed almost 2,000 girls, this was the only death. The NUWSS' response to the report is also in the book. In a bulletin dated 12 December 1916 they question the doctor's statement and point out that that in the six months ending in October 1916, 41 munitions workers had died as a result of TNT poisoning.

Land girls often had little experience of country life – this woman leading a bull looks a little nervous.

Women's Land Army

At home there were more changes to come in the type of work done by women. The large numbers of young men who volunteered to join up at the start of the war left farms bereft of workers at the very time when the need for home grown food increased. Poor women living in the country, like their urban sisters, were expected to work for their living but their roles were clearly defined. Butter making, keeping chickens, milking and haymaking were acceptable tasks for women but the heavier jobs, such as ploughing, were traditionally done by men.

In 1916 the Board of Trade sent organisers around the country to persuade farmers to accept women as agricultural workers on their farms. In January 1917, in order to boost recruitment, the Women's Land Army, organised by the Ministry of Agriculture, replaced the Women's Land Service Corps. To encourage women to enrol they held military style rallies across the country and awarded certificates, badges and stripes.

Although many women volunteered to work on the land, many farmers refused to accept them. They argued that women were not strong enough to undertake ploughing and they preferred to find other ways of overcoming their labour shortages. Some called on retired men to come back to plough and in some areas boys of 12 were excused school so they could work on the land. They also considered the wages suggested by the Government were too high and preferred to pay by the hour. In the areas where women were accepted farmers had to concede that women could do the work.

It may be that some of the resistance to taking on women came from farmers' wives who were concerned about having young women, free from parental control and wearing what they would have seen as outlandish clothes, thrust into their tight communities. (Women in the Land Army wore tunics and breeches.) Selection boards seemed to share these doubts as they only chose women who they felt were morally fitted to cope with the job. Women were strictly supervised and rules stressed that they had to be in by 9 p.m. in the winter and 9.30 p.m. in the summer. They were forbidden to smoke in public and were ordered not to keep their hands in their pockets, though of course in many cases little attention was paid to the rules.

Life on the land was difficult, especially for girls who knew nothing of country ways. In an extract from *Forgotten Voices of the Great War* by Max Arthur, Mary Hillyer describes her life as a land girl on an isolated farm. Her day started at 5 a.m. and often did not finish until 9 p.m., which if she stuck to the rules meant she had no chance to go out after work. She also recalled an amusing incident that happened during her training which shows how strange life must have been for girls unused to country life. Asked to take the sow to the boar, she remembers that she carefully walked the sow to the Boar Hotel and left her in the stables there.

According to Mary, most of the girls who trained with her were from good homes who had volunteered in spite of the bad conditions and poor pay. Many were teachers and office workers with no experience whatsoever of working on the land. But they did not all stay long in the job; although Mary worked hard while she was at the farm she soon left, having, as she said, 'stuck it for six months'. Few working class women were prepared to work on the land. Money was more important to girls with no other income or savings and they preferred the higher wages of the factories to the low wages paid to land girls. For a middle class girl joining the Land Army and getting her hands dirty may have seemed like fun. It gave her a chance to leave home and experience a very different way of life, if only temporarily. But for poor girls it smacked of domestic service, which most of them were keen to avoid.

Nursing and medical work

Women doctors responded very quickly to the announcement of war but the authorities were reluctant to take up their offer of help. One War Office official responded to Dr Elsie Inglis' offer to provide teams for mobile hospitals by telling her to go home and sit still. But like so many pioneering women before her, Dr Inglis refused to take 'no' for an answer and, in September 1914, she set up units of the Scottish Women's Hospitals to work with the French, Belgian and Serbian Armies.

Dr Flora Murray and Dr Louisa Garrett Anderson were another two doctors who were determined to do military work. Knowing that their offers of help were likely to be rejected by the British, they by-passed the War Office and went directly to the French Embassy to offer their services. Their offer was gratefully

Edith Cavell (1865–1915)

Edith Cavell was born the daughter of a Norfolk parson in 1865. There was nothing in her early life to indicate that she would end up a national heroine. Like most middle class women in Victorian England, she could have lived quietly at home, kept by her parents. However Edith was not content to live that way and found work as a governess. Later she trained to be a nurse.

At the start of the war she was working in Belgium, running a training hospital. Although she was a member of the Red Cross and therefore committed to neutrality, Edith Cavell became involved in an organisation that helped allied soldiers escape to neutral territory. In all, 200 allied soldiers passed through her clinic to safety. She was betrayed by a Belgian collaborator and arrested. She was found guilty of helping allied soldiers to escape and was sentenced to death. In spite of much diplomatic pressure her sentence was carried out quickly and she was shot on 12 October 1915.

Her death was used as a propaganda tool and recruiting doubled in the immediate weeks following her execution. In Britain she was portrayed as a heroic woman who was simply following her nursing instincts and saving lives. Any question of her being a spy was hotly denied. Yet a file in the National Archives (KV 2/844), which was opened in May 2002, indicates that her activities were less innocent than portrayed at the time. In the file there is a note dated 3 February 1919, which comments, 'say that the British Military Authorities consider it highly undesirable that anything implicating Miss Cavell in matters of espionage should be published until the final settlement with the Germans has been made irrevocable'.

Although at one level her actions refuted the anti-suffragists claim that women could not serve their country at times of war, the fuss over her execution was precisely because she was a woman and therefore deserving of special treatment as a member of the weaker sex.

accepted and they set off for Paris on 14 September 1914 with the Women's Hospital Corps. Dr Elizabeth Garrett Anderson, Louisa's mother, was among those seeing them off. She must have been very moved to see how far women had come in the fifty years since she'd defied convention to become Britain's first woman doctor.

As well as the professional nurses who served in the war, other women volunteered to help nurse the sick and wounded by joining Voluntary Aid Detachments (VADs). Most VAD recruits were middle and upper class women, as the majority of them received no pay. As they were not qualified nurses they were expected to undertake the more menial tasks in the wards. They were often asked to do nursing work, however, and many became skilled at their jobs, but as VADs their skills were not recognised and they received no promotions.

At the outbreak of war the Government was reluctant to send women to the front but after the terrible carnage of the first year it changed its mind. Women over 23 with at least three months experience were sent out to work on the western front. For women who had been protected from the harsh realities of life nursing the war wounded must have been a traumatic experience, yet many of them tended to make light of the hardship. The First Aid Nursing Yeomanry (FANY) was another service that attracted many upper and middle class women to its ranks. FANYs worked close to the front line driving ambulances, and running field hospitals and canteens for the troops. Their work was dangerous and they won many medals for bravery.

The women's auxiliary services

The Women's Army Auxiliary Corps (WAAC) was founded in 1917 in order to release men for duties at the front. The terrible loss of life on the battlefields meant there was a constant demand for more men at the front. There were worries that too many men were tied up in jobs away from the action. It was decided that women could replace soldiers employed as clerks, telephonists, in signals, as cooks and as orderlies. The WAACs served both at home and in France. Women serving in France had to be 23 while women serving at home had to be 18. Women both home and abroad were strictly disciplined.

The rules of the WAAC, which can be seen in a file in National Archives (WO 32/5253), forbade any fraternising between men and women. No married woman was allowed to serve in France if her husband was a soldier there. If she was already there when he was sent to France she would be sent home. Women were forbidden to smoke while on duty and in public places and thoroughfares. They were also forbidden to drink any alcohol unless it was for medicinal purposes.

Emmie Haines (standing) aged 16, in WRNS uniform – she transferred to the WRAF a month later. The First World War provided her with the opportunity to escape from a life in domestic service.

War office officials clearly found dealing with women something of a problem. Another file in the National Archives (WO 32/5252) contains several documents dealing with the issue of uniforms for officers of the WAAC. One problem that created much correspondence was the issue of badges of rank for women who would hold rank equivalent to officers in the Army. At first it was suggested that women should wear the same badges (the crown and star) as their male counterparts but there were strong objections.

It was feared that women wearing the crown and star would create problems and cause confusion. Under military rules any person wearing those badges of office would have to be saluted. The objection to this was that, as women officers were volunteers and not commissioned officers, asking men to salute them would constitute 'an unlawful command'. After much correspondence, which included a letter from Buckingham Palace, it was decided that, instead of the crown and star, women's badges of rank would be the rose and the fleur de lys. It was also decided that, as there was a shortage of metal, women's badges would be embroidered onto their uniforms.

The success of the WAAC led first to the creation of the Women's Royal Naval Service (WRNS) which was founded in November 1917, followed by the Women's Royal Air Force (WRAF) towards the end of the war in 1918.

The services provided many young women with the chance of a better life. Emmie Haines (later Turner) who was born to a poor family in Portsmouth in June 1901 was one of them (see photograph; also pp. 57 and 99). The eldest of 10 children, she was an intelligent girl who, in spite of having to look after her brothers and sisters, did well at school. Her teacher offered to pay for her books if her parents would allow her to continue her education. But her family was too poor to take up the offer and she left school at the age of 13, destined, like so many girls of her class, for a life in domestic service.

Her first job was as a live-in scullery maid in a house in London. Her life there was harsh and as well as having to suffer the menial, back-breaking work she had to endure the bad temper of the cook, who frequently beat her. After a while an

While the cat's away ...

During the war the newspapers were filled with articles decrying the numbers of women drinking in public houses. They called for government action, concerned that now their menfolk were away, women had no one to control them. They claimed that women were neglecting their children and that prostitutes were using public houses for soliciting. Some newspapers even complained that drinking by munitions workers was putting the country at risk. In some places the Defence of the Realm Act, which was passed in 1914 to give the Government emergency power, was used to ban women from public houses.

It is true that many women, especially young and single working class women, had more money and more freedom than they had in the past, but the numbers getting drunk were a small minority. Much of the fuss about the presence of women in public houses seems to have been a reaction against the level of independence that women were gaining because of the war. Men might not be able to resist the government-backed influx of women into male territory in the workplace, but they could resist them intruding into their places of rest and relaxation.

In a file in the National Archives (HO 45/19649), a report by the Chief Constable to the Middlesborough Licensing Committee in 1926 puts the problem of women's wartime drinking into perspective. In his report he includes a chart which shows the number of women convicted for drunkenness between the years 1911 and 1925. While the report admittedly shows the ban imposed in 1916 was effective in reducing convictions, the number convicted, at its highest, was considerably lower than the number of men convicted for the same reason. A second chart shows that in 1915 only 271 women were convicted of an overall total of 1,469.

aunt found her another situation. When she was 16 she joined the WRNS. Her record of service, which is on microfilm in the National Archives, shows that she enrolled on 13 March 1918 and was employed as a steward. A month later on 15 April she transferred to the WRAF, one of the first six girls from her unit to do so. Her service record does not show her date of birth so it is not clear whether they knew how young she was. She left the service on 30 October 1918 but never returned to domestic service.

Women in action

Although women in the auxiliary forces were not allowed to bear arms, at least two Englishwomen served as soldiers in the First World War: one as a regular soldier, later an officer, in the Serbian Army, the second disguised as a man in the Royal Engineers.

On 1 December 1956 *The Times* published the obituary of Flora Sandes, the daughter of a clergyman, who had fought as a soldier during the First World War. In 1915, when women in England were marching for 'the right to serve' in the munitions factories, this extraordinary woman had joined the Serbian Army as a private.

From an early age Flora showed a spirit of adventure. She could ride and shoot and she loved driving so much that she bought an old racing car. When war broke out she went to Serbia with a nursing unit. Later she joined the Serbian Red Cross and then the ambulance section of the 2nd Infantry Regiment, known as the 'Iron' Regiment, where she employed her nursing skills. She later put her shooting skills to use when the regiment was attacked.

Women were allowed to fight in the Serbian Army so, when the ambulances had to be abandoned, Flora enlisted as a private. She fought in many battles and was promoted many times. She was wounded by a hand grenade in 1916 and after being treated in a field hospital, she returned to England on sick leave. She wrote a book about her experiences entitled *An Englishwoman-Sergeant in the Serbian Army*. The Serbians recognised her courage and she was decorated for conspicuous bravery in the field. While on sick leave she raised money for Serbian soldiers and returned to her regiment in 1917. She married and lived abroad until after the Second World War. She settled in Suffolk where she lived until her death aged 80.

Flora Sandes was not the only woman to flout convention by joining the war in a soldier's role. Dorothy Lawrence was an ambitious young woman who was determined that her sex would not interfere with her ambition to become a war correspondent. In 1915, having been rejected by both the War Office and the newspapers, she set off by herself to get to the front. She was only nineteen years old. She had a difficult task ahead of her as women were banned from the combat zone. Undaunted, she travelled to Paris as a tourist where she set about getting a disguise and the necessary papers. Once there, with the help of several soldiers, she acquired a soldier's uniform and a leave pass for a 'Private Denis Smith'. To complete her disguise she had her hair cut very short. At Albert on the Somme, she joined a night patrol of Royal Engineers and worked with them strengthening trenches for nearly two weeks before she was discovered.

Before she was allowed to return to England, the authorities forced her to swear an affidavit preventing her from making her exploits public. Her book *Sapper Dorothy Lawrence: The Only English Woman Soldier* was published after the war in 1919. It was reviewed by the *Times Literary Supplement* which, after commenting 'it is pleasant to read of the politeness of treatment she received', dismissed her exploits with the comment, 'her fighting experiences hardly entitle her to claim a place in the legendary and historical catalogue of individual women fighters'.

Women win the vote

In February 1918 the Government finally accepted the argument for giving the vote to women and included them in the Representation of the People Act. It was, however, a limited victory as only women over 30 could vote. At that time women outnumbered men and the Government had no intention of allowing women to form the majority of the electorate, especially as they had no idea how women would use their vote.

People have often questioned why women won the vote. The official line, and the argument used in the debates, was that women had earned their citizenship by their war effort. Christabel Pankhurst held a very different view. In her opinion, the Government gave way because they did not want to have to deal with renewed militancy once the war ended. A third reason given is that the quiet but persistent campaigning of the NUWSS, and of Mrs Fawcett in particular, had paid off. Although she had encouraged her members to stop their campaign and concentrate their efforts on the challenge of war work, she never ceased in her efforts to convince the Government that they should give women the vote.

However, none of the reasons is sufficient on its own. If the Government was really rewarding war work then they would not have excluded women under 30 as it was largely the younger women who had worked in the factories, tilled the land,

Vera Brittain (1893–1970)

Vera Brittain is probably the most famous of the VADs thanks to her autobiography *A Testament of Youth*, which covers the period from 1900 to 1925. Born to a wealthy family in 1893, had she wanted it her life could have been one of ease. In her diaries, edited by Alan Bishop and published as *Chronicles of Youth*, she describes her early life as being filled with social gatherings, tennis and dancing. Yet her diaries show a great deal of discontent and frustration at the narrowness of the life she was expected to lead and she envied the freedom enjoyed by her brother.

In 1914 she won a scholarship to Somerville College, Oxford. After a year there she left to become a VAD. Her diaries indicate the mood of the country at the start of the war. For, although she became a committed and passionate pacifist in later years, her diaries show that she too was caught up in the romantic ideal of war that saw honour and glory in self sacrifice for one's country. She encouraged Edward, her only brother, to join up much against their father's wishes.

Her experiences as a VAD, together with the loss of her fiancé, her brother and her closest friends, turned her into a pacifist. After the war, though devastated by her personal losses, she returned to Somerville and graduated in 1921. After graduating, she started a career as a writer but her novels were not well received and she turned to journalism. She wrote for the feminist journal *Time and Tide*. During and after the Second World War she criticised the Government for its blanket bombing of urban areas of Germany. She was a strong opponent of nuclear weapons and in the 1950s helped to form CND. She continued to work for peace until her death in 1970.

nursed the sick and wounded and served in the women's military services. It is unlikely that the tactics of quiet persuasion, having failed to make any impression on the Government for over forty years, would have suddenly become irresistible. While early militancy had been effective in winning converts, the Government would not want to be seen to give in to violence. A combination of all three is therefore the most likely explanation. The war gave the Government an excuse to give women the vote without losing face. They needed to rebuild after the war and

The Women's Institute

The Women's Institute (WI), long renowned for its jam-making and cake stalls at village fetes, first appeared in Britain during the First World War. The WI originated in Canada, founded in 1897 by Adelaide Hoodless, a campaigner for the practical education for women. Its aims were to provide women in rural areas with the opportunity to meet together to combat loneliness and to share ideas. Encouraged by the Canadian provincial governments, who saw its social and educational value, the WI was soon a feature of rural areas throughout Canada. The movement soon spread from Canada to the USA and into Europe.

The first British WI was founded on 11 September 1915 in a small village in Anglesey, Wales, with the encouragement of the Agricultural Organisations Society. One of its strengths was that it was non-sectarian and non-political and by the end of the year it had several branches in Wales and had spread to England. Within two years responsibility for the British WI was taken by the Women's Section of the Food Department of the Board of Agriculture, which recognised the part that the WI could play in the war effort. Although in Canada the WI's role had been mainly social and educational, in Britain its wartime role was to utilise the skills of rural married women, whose family commitments prevented them from volunteering for other work. WIs encouraged women to keep chickens and pigs, grow food in their gardens and in small-holdings, preserve food, and knit clothing for the troops.

The WI was also to play an important role during the Second World War especially in the preservation of food. With food shortages acute, the ability of the WI to mobilise large numbers of women across the country in preservation centres proved a godsend whenever there was a glut of fruit that needed to be bottled or made into jam. Before the war ended they were to produce many thousands of tons of preserves. Since the war they have been involved in a number of campaigns to protect the countryside and its way of life. Their most recent causes include campaigning to keep rural post offices open and to limit the use of harmful chemicals in farming.

they needed to do so in a period of stability without further agitation from the suffragists and suffragettes.

Demobilisation

At the end of the war a great effort was made to persuade women to return to their traditional roles. No doubt many welcomed the return to normality. Women who worked in munitions and workers on the land had known from the start that their work would end with the war. After the war many men, and some women, felt that it was a woman's patriotic duty to return to her home and do her part in repopulating the country.

Yet even though many women had to relinquish their jobs, life in Britain would never be the same again. During the war many women had become heads of households, had managed finances and had learned to make decisions for themselves. They had succeeded in a number of jobs formerly thought to be beyond their capabilities. Some had won the right to vote. Even those who returned to their traditional roles of wife and mother were less likely to accept the submissiveness expected of them before the war.

Single women in the upper and middle classes who had won their independence during the war years were reluctant to return to being dutiful daughters kept by their fathers. Vera Brittain (see profile, p.47) summed up the feelings of many when she wrote in *Testament of Youth*, 'I had always known, and my parents had always tolerantly taken for granted, that … my return to a position of subservient dependence at home would be tolerable neither for them nor for me'.

During the war clothing became simpler and less restrictive, and this also had an impact on women's lives. Skirts, which in the Edwardian period had swept the floor, became shorter. The regulation length of a WAAC's skirt was 8½ inches above the ground at home, while in France it was 9 inches above the ground. As long skirts made it difficult for women serving as tram conductors to go up and down the stairs, the skirts of their uniforms were shortened to mid-calf length.

Wartime dress had been born of necessity and reflected the more active lives of women. While it was sombre and functional it was more comfortable and enabled the wearer to move more freely. Just as many young women would not go back to accepting the old order in their social lives, dispensing with chaperones and insisting on independence, they rejected the corsets and restrictive clothing of the pre-war years. The fashions of the next decade would reflect the attitudes of the women who had come of age, in more ways than one, during the First World War.

The 'modern miss'

Freedom ... and self-support ... were the only conditions in which ...
a post Victorian woman could do her work and maintain self-respect.

VERA BRITTAIN, FROM TESTAMENT OF YOUTH

The popular image of the 1920s woman is that of the 'flapper'; a freedom-loving, social butterfly for whom life in the 'roaring twenties' was a social whirl of never-ending parties, tennis and fun. These 'bright young things' defied convention in all manner of ways: they smoked openly and drank cocktails. They horrified their elders and dazzled young men by wearing shockingly short and often backless dresses. They threw away their corsets, bound their breasts and chopped off their hair. First they reduced their 'crowning glory' to a mere bob and then went even further and had it cut into the severe and boyish Eton crop. Flappers danced until dawn taking great pleasure in such outrageous dances as the Black Bottom and the Charleston. They lived in flats, drove their own cars and the most daring of them learned to fly.

While this image of the 1920s sophisticate was only true of a few wealthy women, the war had brought changes in women's dress and behaviour which worried a number of people. What concerned many of the older generation was what they saw as the breakdown of the old social conventions especially among the 'respectable' classes. Single women, who had tended wounded men, risked their lives in munitions factories and worked in all weathers on the land, all without a chaperone, were not going to relinquish their freedom easily. Women who had lived in hostels and shared flats during the war were not prepared to sit at home doing nothing while waiting for marriage to rescue them from the parental home. They had tasted independence and, while an eventual marriage might curtail it, many of them were determined that they would not return to their old subservient lives as dutiful daughters.

One reason given at the time for the social upheaval was the large imbalance in the population resulting from wartime losses. *The Times*, dated 5 December 1920, reported on a lecture given at the Institute of Hygiene by a Dr Murray-Leslie, who discussed the problems arising from what he referred to as the existence of 'over 1,000,000 excess females of reproductive age'. He bemoaned the lack of parental supervision and the freedom of the 'modern independent girl', decrying her interest in 'pleasure for pleasure's sake'. He continued in this vein and blamed 'her rebellion against convention and discipline' for the decline in moral standards.

According to Dr Murray-Leslie, women fell into one of three types: the domestic, the intellectual and the social butterfly. He had little to say about the domestic type, other than that she was rare in the upper and middle classes. He dismissed the purely intellectual woman as 'not usually sexually attractive' but condescended to say that the intelligent, well-read woman who also 'appreciated the charms of dress refinement, and other social amenities' was the best fitted for marriage. He reserved his condemnation for the type he called the attractive, social butterfly with 'strong reproductive instincts'. He believed that this type of woman, by competing for male attention, was corrupting men. He accused them of failing to elevate a man's ideals and of striving 'by means of dress or the lack of it to appeal to man's lower nature'. He assured his audience that it was the shameless behaviour of these predatory, single women that led to men's infidelity and their consequent unhappy marriages.

His views, and those of others like him, must have been an anathema to the women who had put so much into the war effort. For there was a dark side to the fun and frivolity: many were in denial, using the parties and the dancing as a way of forgetting, if only for a short while, the horrors they had experienced and the losses they had endured as a result of the war. This is poignantly illustrated by

OPPOSITE
Although this picture is dated
1931, it shows typical twenties
fashions – as well as something
of women's growing
independence.

THE BROADS
200 MILES OF SAFE INLAND WATERWAYS

HOLIDAYS AFLOAT £4 PER WEEK
BOOKLET FREE FROM PASSENGER MANAGER, LIVERPOOL STREET STATION. LONDON E.C.2. OR ANY L·N·E·R ENQUIRY OFFICE.
PARTICULARS OF YACHTS FOR HIRE FROM NORFOLK BROADS BUREAU. 22 NEWGATE STREET. LONDON. E.C.1.

This 1926 poster advertising expensive holidays shows that life could be good for upper class women in the 1920s – but many of them partied to forget the horrors of the First World War. Others, meanwhile, campaigned to extend voting rights to all women over 21.

Vera Brittain's reaction to the sudden death of a university friend, which she described in *Testament of Youth*. She wrote that after hearing the news, 'I pushed the thought of her away and flung myself furiously into Mary's tennis parties, for I was sick beyond description of death and loss'.

Dr Murray Leslie was also over reacting when he referred to women's skimpy dress. He was probably alarmed because ankles, which had been covered up during the Victorian and Edwardian eras, were now on full view. The majority of women in the 1920s wore dresses and skirts that were a respectable calf length, only a few inches shorter than the length of a WAAC's uniform. The 1920s style, with its dropped waist, flat chest and emphasis on straight lines, played down a woman's curves. The clothes usually associated with the 1920s flapper were the party clothes worn by wealthy, fashionable women, and even then the shorter skirts were not in vogue until late into the decade.

Not all women accepted the changes in dress and some, the older ones in particular, clung to the pre-war styles. From a photograph taken in 1920, it is clear that Emily English, my great-grandmother (see photograph), was among those who kept to the old style. She was not the only woman to resist the newer fashions. On 21 June 1927 in a section headed 'News in brief' *The Times* reported on the findings of an inquest in Camberwell, London. The deceased, a Mrs Elizabeth Cotterell had tripped over her long skirts and had died of her subsequent injuries; she had, apparently, objected to short skirts. The inquest recorded a verdict of accidental death.

It was not only in the outward appearances that life in the 1920s differed from the popular image. Far from enjoying a fun-filled social whirl, many women faced an uncertain future. For a large number of them, the war had brought a great deal of heartache and financial uncertainty. The statistic of almost 1,000,000 men killed translated into fathers, brothers, husbands and sons lost in the war. Some women lost their fiancés and never married. The loss of a breadwinner affected all classes. Some aristocratic families were impoverished when a man was killed soon after succeeding to his father's title, thereby incurring a second set of death duties as the estate passed to the next male heir. Widows, and those with husbands too badly injured to work, struggled to keep their families. Many single women faced a future in which they would have to support themselves and, in some cases, their ageing parents. Women like Vera Brittain wanted the challenge of earning their living; others had it thrust upon them.

The author's great-grandmother, Emily English (née Bennett) in 1920.

Women and work

For the well-educated woman, the start of the 1920s seemed to hold great promise. The principle of votes for women had been conceded, if not fully implemented, and a woman sat in the House of Commons. Equally important, Parliament had passed the Sex Disqualification (Removal) Act in 1919. Under the terms of this Act it was unlawful to refuse a woman entry to the professions on the grounds of her sex and as a result many new opportunities were, in theory at least, presented to women. Banking, accountancy, law and engineering were among the new professions now open. The priesthood and the floor of the Stock Exchange, however, remained exclusively male provinces.

The marriage bar

By the 1920s, the Victorian idea that a woman's place was in the home was dead. Dead that is for single women. In spite of the Sex Disqualification (Removal) Act which was supposed to remove the barriers against women working, married or otherwise, pressure was put on married women to return to the home. To ensure that they did, many employers, including the civil service and local government, created a marriage bar. They refused to employ married women and forced their female employees to resign as soon as they married. Women teachers, nurses and doctors were among those that lost their jobs in this way.

Although some women campaigned against the marriage bar, many accepted it. In the 1920s, marriage and motherhood was still seen as a job in itself, and the idea that a woman should be at home to care for her husband and family was well entrenched. Many believed that a married woman had no right to work as she had a husband to provide for her. At a time when men were expected to support their wives and children, few women would argue for the employment of married women while there were men unemployed. In a period of job shortages some also felt that the marriage bar benefited single women. In an example given in *Women in Britain Since 1900* by Sue Bruley, a married woman met with a great deal of resentment from the girls in her office for taking a job which they considered could have gone to a single girl. As a result, she left but, needing the money, she found another job, this time pretending to be single.

She was not the only woman to have kept her marriage hidden in order to keep working. In *Out of the Doll's House*, Angela Holdsworth gives examples of women who lied about their marital status to keep their jobs. One was Janet Robson, who married Stewart Young in 1935 but told nobody as she couldn't afford to give up work. When her husband's financial position improved, they married again as if for the first time. It is interesting to note that, although Janet had been employed before and after her first marriage, neither of her marriage certificates gives her rank or profession; she is merely noted as being a spinster.

In 1920, in response to the Sex Disqualification (Removal) Act, Oxford University awarded degrees to its women students. In *Testament of Youth*, Vera Brittain, who was at Oxford at the time, recalls the ceremony and the huge cheers given to the first women to receive their degrees. On 11 May 1922, *The Times* reported that one of those graduates, Dr Ivy Williams, had become the first woman to be called to the English bar. Women in the past, Christabel Pankhurst among them, had passed the exams necessary to qualify as a barrister but, because they were women, they had not been allowed to practise. Christabel, however, was able to use her knowledge of the law on the occasions she found herself in court as a result of her militancy.

While employers made changes to accommodate the new law, conditions were often imposed which made it difficult for women to progress in the professions. One of the offenders was the Government itself. On 6 August 1921, *The Times* reported on changes in the admission of women to the Civil Service. The Government announced that, at a time within three years, women would be admitted to the Civil Service, with 'the mode of admission ... the same for both sexes'. So far so good, but it added that the Civil Service Commissioners were expected to 'pay due regard for suitability in the allocation of successful candidates', which left the field open for discrimination. The Government admitted as much by stating that women would not receive the same pay as men, as this would cost too much. It also conceded that there might be 'traces of discrimination' but claimed that they were there in women's interests. It no doubt felt it was in women's interest to debar them from overseas postings in the Foreign Office.

The Times ran a more encouraging report when it covered the International Conference of Women in Science, Industry and Commerce, which was held at Wembley on 16 January 1925. Miss C. Criff, who presided at the conference, was enthusiastic about the advances that women had made. She reported that women now held good positions in engineering and in science in both the technical and the executive areas. In support of her claim, she said that in London there was an engineering firm staffed by women and a steel company directed by women. She added that women were doing even better in the sciences. A more cautious line was taken by a Miss E. Wilson who said that the problem of male unemployment, together with traditional views of what was appropriate work for women, was making it difficult for women to succeed in engineering. She felt that an upturn in the economy was needed if women were to enter the profession in any numbers.

Miss Criff's enthusiasm and Miss Wilson's caution, though seeming to be contradictory, were both justified. There was indeed cause for celebration when a woman succeeded in entering what traditionally was a male profession. But there was no room for complacency either, as another report from *The Times* shows. Although women had been doctors since the Victorian period, male resistance to women in medicine remained strong. As late as March 1928, *The Times* reported that several London hospitals were threatening to exclude women medical students. Those that were already there would be allowed to finish their course but no new female students would be admitted. *The Times* gave a number of reasons for this course of action. The most bizarre, which it appeared to take seriously, was that mixed colleges were worried that by admitting women they were reducing the number of men available for their sports teams. They were also concerned that keen sportsmen might be reluctant to apply to mixed colleges.

While in theory women were gaining new opportunities for work, larger numbers of them were facing unemployment. Munitions workers had known from the start that their jobs were only for the duration of the war but many of them lost their jobs sooner. Other wartime jobs were also earmarked for returning servicemen and women were forced out of them as soon as men returned. In some cases qualified and experienced women who had taken examinations had to give up their jobs to unqualified and less experienced men.

Unemployed women in a dole queue, c.1929. As unemployment grew, many single girls favoured the marriage bar and resented working wives – especially as it was commonly believed that they only worked for 'pin money' for themselves or to provide luxuries for their families.

In order to keep down unemployment the Government, employers and trade unions worked together to push women back into their pre-war roles. Married women were actively discouraged from working and most single women who were working at the time of their marriage were expected to resign or were sacked. Single, working class women were pushed back into domestic service and the Government ran 'homecraft' courses to encourage the idea that domestic service was a worthwhile job.

With growing unemployment amongst women and few training schemes, the only job option for the majority of women after the war was in domestic service. During the 1920s domestic service was still the largest employer of women but in most cases it was entered into unwillingly and many women refused to return to a life of drudgery. Before the war domestic service was, in most areas, thought to be a cut above factory work, but after the war the position was largely reversed. Women who had received the higher wages paid by factories and enjoyed the freedom of not being at someone's beck and call at all hours now preferred factory work. During the war thousands of women had left domestic service to take up work in a variety of other better-paid occupations. Parlourmaids, for example, found more lucrative work as waitresses in cafes, teashops and restaurants. As early as 9 June 1915, *The Times*, after reporting on the reasons for the wartime shortage of parlourmaids, had questioned whether women would be prepared to return to domestic service on the old terms once the war was over.

It was not just the low pay and longer hours that put women off domestic service. During the war many women had gained self-respect from knowing that their work was vital to the survival of the country. Workers outside domestic service mixed with a wide range of people, including friends, and after work their time was their own. Life in domestic service was very different. As servants they were treated as though their only purpose in life was to serve their employers. Their lives were strictly controlled and, unless they had time off, they were not allowed to leave the premises without permission. During the evenings they would have to sit long hours in a kitchen with only the other servants for company. If their employer could only afford one maid then, as well as the extra work, they also faced the problems of loneliness. On top of that they were expected to show due deference to their employer. It is little wonder that many women who had experienced the liberating atmosphere of the war years did not want to return to a life of servitude.

Emmie Haines was one of the girls who, made more confident by her time in the WRNS and the WRAF, rejected the return to domestic service. After the war, she found a live-in job as a shop assistant in Bourne and Hollingsworth, a

The Government's solution to women's rising unemployment in the 1920s was to offer them training as domestics in centres like this one in Market Harborough.

department store in London, and enrolled in evening classes where she gained qualifications in shorthand and typing. Her daughter Betty remembers her mother telling her that she existed on a glass of milk and a penny bun a day so that she could afford the classes. Soon after qualifying, she returned home and found a job locally as a shorthand typist. She was able to help support her widowed mother and younger brothers and sisters. But like so many women she had to give up her job as soon as she married.

Shortage of alternative jobs, however, meant that many women did re-enter domestic service, though in fewer numbers. But those that did return were less likely to stay long in a job they found uncongenial. In a letter to *The Times* in 1927 a housemaster of an unnamed school wrote to complain about the servants' agencies that he believed were exploiting employers. He alleged that, although he had paid the agency a fee for a housemaid and had paid the girl's fare to the school, she had walked out after only six days. He said that the agency claimed it had no other permanent staff available and instead offered him temporary help, which cost him another fee.

Problems in recruiting domestics may have come from competition among employers. Advertisements for cooks in the same issue of *The Times* show that employers were offering inducements to attract staff. While an agency offered a cook £52 a year, private individuals were offering a good deal more. One advertisement offered £75 plus liberal outings and own bedroom. Another offered 'high wages' while a third offered 'good wages' and 'outings', and emphasised that the cook would be helped by a kitchen and a scullery maid. In another advertisement a parlourmaid was offered £50 a year, adding that very little housework was involved and that five other servants were employed in the house. It is not clear whether this inducement was to stress that the work would be light or to alleviate the spectre of loneliness that put off many domestics from applying to be a maid in a house with only one servant.

Love, marriage and motherhood

After the war women not only rejected the role of the kept, subservient daughter; some of them also rejected the role of the kept, subservient wife. Having tasted independence they wanted something more than the traditional marriage in which women were content with a purely domestic role. Many spoke of an ideal marriage as a companionable partnership with both members equally valued. Vera Brittain wrote in *Testament of Youth*, 'I knew a growing number of women who would refuse marriage rather than give themselves up to years of exclusive domesticity and throw away their training and experience'.

Alexandra Reilly, my mother (see photograph), was one of those who rebelled against the life that was planned out for her. Although she had been educated and could speak several languages, she was not expected to earn her own living. Ever independent, she made an informal arrangement with her old school whereby she taught part time in exchange for shorthand and typing lessons. When she found a job in an office her father, whose views on the role of women were distinctly Victorian, was mortified. He claimed that she had disgraced him by working, as people thought he could not afford to keep his family. An indulgent father, he was hurt that she preferred to earn her own living to accepting an allowance from him. Her rebellion went further, and she refused a number of proposals from suitably wealthy men who her father considered would make good husbands. When asked why she refused to marry a man who would have kept her in luxury, she replied, with a touch of defiance, 'I didn't want to be a bird in a golden cage'.

The author's mother, Alexandra Reilly (née Wakim). This photograph was taken sometime in the 1930s. Her glamorous looks belied a fiercely independent spirit.

The idea of marriage as an equal partnership was taken even further by Marie Stopes (see profile, p. 62). In her book, *Married Love*, published in 1918, she claimed that equality in marriage included a woman's right to enjoy sexual love. She believed that, contrary to current ideas, women could and should enjoy sex within a marriage. She also argued that it was up to a husband to awaken his chaste wife to the pleasures of sexual love. Her book provoked outrage. A file in the National Archives on the 'Dr Hannah Brown' case (see p. 63), contains a note on a report from the London City Police Commissioners which refers to Marie Stopes as a 'fraud and humbug so far as her books are concerned. They are simply best sellers in pornography ...'.

For years the church had taught that enjoyment of sex without intending to procreate was sinful even within marriage. By the standards of the time, only depraved women enjoyed sex, which is why a woman's adultery was seen as so reprehensible. Marie Stopes challenged that view. The 1923 change in the divorce law, which gave women the same rights to divorce as a man, was considered by some as an attack on existing moral standards. Implicit in the change was the belief that adultery on the part of a husband was as bad as that of a wife. Several MPs rejected this concept and argued against changing the law. *The Times*, 3 May, gives some of the opposing MPs' objections. One asked, 'Was there any member of the House ... who would regard the sin of adultery by his son in the same light as the sin of adultery by his daughter?' Another objected on the grounds that a man's adultery 'did not introduce a bastard into the household of his wife. If a woman were an adulterer she made the man the legal father of a bastard'.

The possibility of a companionable, sexually fulfilling marriage in which each was an equal partner was a dream few could realise. Only women in the upper classes who, in general, tended to have fewer children, to say nothing of paid help, would have found it feasible to break with tradition to such an extent. And even they were hampered in their desire for financial independence by the existence of the marriage bar. For women with large families, living in cramped, hard to clean housing with little money for the basic necessities, let alone servants, the whole idea would have been laughable.

While a few women were searching for a marriage of equals, the majority still saw marriage as a means to children and a home of their own. Some saw motherhood as the highest expression of a woman's nature. Government propaganda elevated motherhood to a patriotic duty, something few disagreed with after the huge loss of life in the war. Even Vera Brittain, who was determined not to settle for anything less in marriage than a partnership of equals, wrote that the country needed 'its more vigorous and intelligent women to be the mothers of the generations to come'.

During the war concern about the loss of life and the effect on the population affected attitudes towards illegitimacy. In May 1916, the *Westminster Gazette* reported the views of Ronald MacNeil who claimed that the large number of illegitimate children in areas where troops had been stationed (he mentioned 2,000 in one county borough alone) was a blessing in disguise. He appealed for a more forgiving attitude towards the mothers and claimed that many of the men concerned had paid for their sin with their lives. He pleaded that the mothers should not be punished for their 'single lapse from virtue' and asked for help to be given to the children so that they could grow up to be healthy and a credit to the country.

During the war the National Council for the Unmarried Mother and her Child was initially formed to campaign for reform of the Bastardy Acts. In 1918 and in 1923 the Government passed laws increasing the maximum payments made to mothers of illegitimate children. Three years later, in 1926, it passed a Legitimacy Act, which removed the stigma of illegitimacy from a child whose parents subsequently married. Yet in spite of this apparent relaxation in attitudes, a daughter with an illegitimate child still brought shame to a family. If a single mother had no one to care for her she could be sent to a mental institution under laws which classed women who became pregnant outside marriage as 'feeble minded'. Once committed she was likely to remain there for the rest of her life. Others were sent to the workhouse.

Ever since the Boer War, when many men had been too unhealthy and unfit to join the services, the Government had taken an interest in motherhood. Instead of blaming the conditions in which the poor lived, it tended to blame bad mothers. While it is true that many women did not follow hygienic procedures in caring for their children, that was due as much to the lack of facilities in their homes as it was to deliberate neglect. At the end of the First World War clinics were opened which provided health advice free to mothers. It was part of the campaign to improve the health of children but at the same time it elevated the status of mothers, stressing their importance to the nation.

Although many in authority were keen to increase the birth rate after the war, women were rightly concerned about the high risk of pregnancy. In the 1920s, the number of women dying in childbirth increased. More women were having their babies in hospital where puerperal sepsis spread more rapidly. Even those who coped with childbirth were exhausted by repeated pregnancies. In the same period, more babies were surviving into childhood, which put an added burden on families who faced overcrowding and increased poverty as a result. It is little wonder that, rather than embrace their patriotic duty to have large families, women were seeking ways to limit the number of their pregnancies.

Birth control

While some upper and middle class women were concerned with issues like equal pay, the ending of the marriage bar and extending voting rights to all women, others put their energies into the more controversial issue of birth control. For a large number of women the greatest restriction on their freedom came from the number of pregnancies that they endured. Birth control campaigners realised that there could be no real improvement in the lives of poorer women until they had the means to control the size of their family.

Although upper and middle class women tended to have smaller families and were likely to have used some methods of birth control, the subject still met with strong opposition in the 1920s. When Marie Stopes followed her book on marriage with one entitled *Wise Parenthood* in 1918, there was a huge outcry. Her second book, recognising that the main obstacle to the enjoyment of sex within marriage was the fear of pregnancy, advocated the use of birth control. In 1921 she went further and opened the first British birth control clinic in Holloway, North London.

Some who objected to birth control did so on religious grounds, while others seemed concerned about the effects it would have on an already falling birth rate. It seems that in some cases objections were part of a wider resentment to women's changing role. A note on the 'Dr Hannah Brown' case in the National Archives file (see p. 63) has the comment, 'It is rather a sign of the times that married women should decline to accept the responsibilities of motherhood, notwithstanding the state gives so much assistance to parents'. Publishing information on birth control could bring prosecution under the obscenity laws. In 1923 Dora Russell was prosecuted for publishing a leaflet which contained a diagram showing how to insert a diaphragm.

Marie Stopes (1880–1958)

Marie Stopes was born in Edinburgh in 1880. Her father was a scientist and her mother a committed feminist. Marie won a science scholarship to London University where she gained her BSc. She went on to gain a DSc in 1905 and became Britain's youngest doctor of science. Marie Stopes' first marriage was annulled for non-consummation in 1916, and it was this experience that led her to write her book, *Married Love*. The book was a huge success and had to be reprinted several times. It was published in America but was banned as being obscene.

Marie's next book, *Wise Parenthood*, was even more controversial as it discussed the taboo topics of birth control and abortion. She had to be careful how she wrote as in the past anyone who had dared to tackle the subject had been sentenced to prison. She was condemned by both the Anglican and Catholic churches for her views. In 1923 she brought a libel case against a Catholic doctor who alleged that she was experimenting on the poor in her clinics. She won the case but the verdict was overturned the following year by the House of Lords.

In 1921 she set up the Society for Constructive Birth Control and on 17 March 1921, with the financial support of her second husband, Humphrey Verdun-Roe, she opened Britain's first birth control clinic in Holloway, London. She also wrote for the newspaper *Birth Control News*.

In spite of the obvious risks of repeated pregnancies to a woman's health, neither the Government nor the medical profession was prepared to act. Opposition from the church was strong and this made the Government unwilling to risk incurring their wrath and the likely affect on the electorate. An attempt to pass a birth control law in 1926 was defeated by nervous politicians. It is more difficult, however, to understand the attitude of the medical establishment. When women asked for advice on birth control at the Maternity and Child Welfare clinics they were refused. Clinics were not allowed to give advice on birth control even if another pregnancy would endanger a woman's life. In such cases, the official Ministry of Health line was that such a woman should be referred to a private practitioner or a hospital.

In correspondence in a file in the National Archives (MH 79/263), the Ministry of Health gave two reasons for its stance. The first was that if birth control advice was freely available at the clinics mothers would stay away; it also argued that as the clinics were funded by public money they should not involve themselves in controversial issues. However the claims that advice was being given by clinics may have been true in some places. The health visitor in Edmonton who was sacked for giving birth control advice is unlikely to have been the only woman who was moved enough by the plight of the mothers to risk her job.

In the absence of reliable birth control methods, many women used abortion as a means of avoiding unwanted pregnancies. Marie Stopes claimed that many uneducated women, not knowing the difference between contraception and abortion, had written to her for advice on abortion, not realising that it was illegal. The National Archives file on the 'Dr Hannah Brown' case (HO 45/24782) shows that in 1927, Marie Stopes complained to the Government about the Le Brassseur Surgical Co. Ltd, who were using her name in publicity material to promote the sale of pills that were intended to induce abortions. Once the Government investigation showed that the pills advertised were harmless, nothing further was done and the Home Office commented, 'It would be difficult, I think, to draw any distinction between Miss Stopes' own practices and methods and those of the firms she denounces'.

The comment showed a lack of compassion for the women duped by firms who preyed on their dread of an unwanted pregnancy. In the 1920s many unscrupulous firms advertised pills claiming to correct 'irregularities' in a woman's cycle. Women recognised the code and would buy them if they suspected they were pregnant. Often the pills were harmless, deliberately so: if they failed to induce a miscarriage, the firm could not be charged with breaking the law. It was also a ruse to make money as pills were sold in different strengths with the price linked to their supposed strength. When the weaker pills failed to work, the unsuspecting woman would be offered a stronger one at a higher price.

The Government did, however, act on Marie Stopes' allegation that 'Dr Hannah Brown', who advertised in the press, was not a doctor but an abortionist. Investigations revealed that the 'doctor' was in fact a front for the supply of abortifacients. The case was reported in the press when it was discovered that one of the people behind the bogus doctor was the Rev. Francis Bacon, Church of England vicar of All Saints. In this case the pills sold were genuine and dangerous. The file on the 'Dr Hannah Brown' case describes some of the horrifying 'treatments' that women were prepared to undergo in order to avoid pregnancy. They make uncomfortable reading and indicate how desperate some women must have been to avoid pregnancy. According to the report in the file, most of the women seeking abortions were married. It was to stop women from having to resort to such measures to limit the size of their families that women were campaigning so hard for birth control.

Women MPs and Parliament

In November 1918, three weeks before the general election, the Parliament (Qualification of Women) Act was passed which enabled women to stand as candidates for Parliament. The timing of the Act meant that women had little time to organise themselves and, as a result, only seventeen women stood for election. Constance Markievicz, who stood for Sinn Fein in Dublin and was therefore almost guaranteed election, was the only successful woman. Among the first MPs, Lady Astor (see profile), Margaret Wintringham, and Mabel Philipson were elected in constituencies previously held by their husbands. By 1923 women were being elected in constituencies where they had no family connections.

Although there were only a few women MPs, throughout the 1920s laws were passed to improve women's lives. As well as laws on legitimacy and maintenance, other laws included equality in divorce, the raising of the age of consent to sixteen,

Lady Astor during the election campaign in her constituency of Plymouth, 1923.

Lady Astor (1879–1964)

It is ironic that Lady Astor, the first woman to take her seat in the House of Commons, was an American who had never been involved in the struggle to win the vote. Nancy Astor was born on 19 May 1879 in Virginia, USA. She came to England in 1904 and in 1906 married Waldorf Astor, her second husband. In 1919, he inherited his father's title and took his seat in the House of Lords. Lady Astor stood in her husband's place at the ensuing by-election and was duly elected Conservative MP for Plymouth Sutton.

In spite of her political connections she found that she was not welcome in the Commons. Winston Churchill was one of those who resented her 'intrusion' into what had always been an all-male environment. In June 1964, an article in the *Sunday Times Magazine* about women politicians quoted him as saying that he was as embarrassed by her presence in the Commons 'as if she had burst into his bathroom when he had nothing to defend himself with but a sponge'. His obvious resentment and irritation failed to intimidate Lady Astor who put him down with the retort that he was '... not handsome enough to have worries of that kind'.

Lady Astor's maiden speech was in favour of temperance and in 1923 she successfully put forward a private member's bill to increase the age qualification for the purchase of alcohol to 18. She was interested in social reform, especially the protection of children, and campaigned for equal voting rights with men as well as equal rights for women in the civil service. In spite of her own divorce and her interest in equal rights she voted against the reform of the divorce laws. She also opposed the spread of information on birth control, believing that it would lead to a lowering of women's morals.

and improvements in women's rights to their children. Even if the number of women MPs was too small to affect legislation directly, the fact that there were now women voters must have had an effect on Parliament's thinking. It justified the arguments of women like Mrs Pankhurst who had always insisted that once women had the vote the Government would pay more attention to their welfare. In 1928, after more than 60 years of hard campaigning, women finally achieved full recognition as citizens when they were granted the vote on the same terms as men.

In the following year, fourteen women were elected to Parliament and Margaret Bondfield, who had served as a parliamentary secretary in the 1924 government, became the first woman cabinet minister when she was made Minister of Labour. Although women in the House of Commons had a difficult time with poor facilities and many men refusing to take them seriously, many must have thought that the changes at the end of the decade heralded a brighter future.

Domestic bliss or suburban neurosis?

The tradition of woman as home-maker encumbers her intellectual and economic progress at every turn.

WINIFRED HOLTBY

Two contrasting images spring to mind in connection with the 1930s. The first is of the Depression with its mass unemployment, hardship and hunger; the second is of tree-lined suburbia with its neat gardens and happy families. Another aspect of the 1930s is the lower profile of women. In the earlier decades of the century, the suffragettes, the war workers and the flappers were all in the public eye. Yet in the 1930s women, with a few notable exceptions, seem to have disappeared, eclipsed by economic problems in the first case and hidden behind net curtains in the second.

In keeping with the more subdued times, the 1930s saw a return to a new femininity. The androgynous look of the 1920s disappeared as longer hair became fashionable and women claimed back their curves. Clothes were more restrained and skirts lengthened. Under the influence of Hollywood films, glamour and make-up were becoming acceptable, though many men were opposed to their daughters wearing it. In their minds a 'painted woman' was a harlot. One father, when his daughter said that she wanted to train as a milliner retorted, 'what, work in that shop, the next thing I know is that you'll be wearing lipstick and painting your nails'. He sent her to commercial college instead.

For a large number of women, fashion and make-up, or even equal rights for that matter, were the furthest things from their minds. For them the pressing problem was one of survival as the economic depression took hold of the country. Women in the hardest hit areas, the North, industrial Scotland and South Wales, struggled to keep their families on the low level of benefits paid to the unemployed. Men in the heavy industries were the worst hit by unemployment; in some of these areas their wives could still find jobs, but the family was plunged into poverty as women rarely earned a living wage. This switching of roles created problems in many homes. Skilled, unemployed men did not take kindly to the added humiliation of being forced to live on a wife's meagre earnings.

'Red Ellen' Wilkinson (see profile, p. 68), MP for Jarrow, brought much needed publicity to the problems suffered by the unemployed in the northern towns when she joined the Jarrow March to London in 1936. At the end of the march, she presented a petition from the people of Jarrow to Parliament asking for government help to combat unemployment, but nothing was done. Although she had the highest profile, she was not the only woman to protest at government inaction.

Many women joined marches organised by the National Unemployed Workers' Movement to protest against unemployment. Male leaders initially rejected the idea of women marching but they relented and allowed separate women's marches. One determined woman, Maggie Nelson, a weaver from Lancashire, marched for 250 miles carrying a heavy backpack. In some areas, where there was no alternative accommodation, women slept in workhouses along the route. For some, conditions on the marches were worse. In *A Century of Women*, Sheila Rowbotham quotes a Mary Docherty who recalls women on the 1933 Scottish Hunger March being forced to sleep on the pavements.

Women in the Depression

It was not only the working classes who felt the effects of the Depression. Some in the upper classes saw the value of their investments wiped out and were

'Red Ellen' Wilkinson, MP (1891–1947)

'Red Ellen' Wilkinson, so called for a combination of her left-wing views, fiery temperament and red hair, is probably best known for her involvement with the Jarrow march to London in 1936. At the time, she was the town's MP and did her best to bring its plight to the authorities. Later she wrote a book about Jarrow, *The Town that was Murdered*. Her concern with the poor is not surprising, as she was an active campaigner on a number of issues before becoming an MP.

Ellen was born into a working class family in Manchester in 1891. At that time few working class girls received more than the most basic education, yet she succeeded in gaining a number of scholarships which led eventually to her winning a place at Manchester University. She was interested in politics from an early age and was a committed suffragist. It would have been interesting to note her reaction if, while she was busy working for the National Union of Women's Suffrage Societies, she had been told that not only would women have the vote but that she would end up as a cabinet minister.

Ellen never forgot her roots and throughout her life she was concerned with the lot of the poor and underprivileged in society. She became involved with the trade union movement and was the first woman organiser of the Amalgamated Union of Co-operative Employees. She was a councillor on Manchester City Council where she argued for women's rights and help for the unemployed. She first became an MP in 1924 and continued her campaigns in Parliament. The poor especially welcomed her Hire Purchase Act 1938, which helped to curb the growing number of goods that were repossessed.

In 1945 she became the first woman Minister for Education. During her time in the cabinet she attempted to raise the school leaving age to 16, and brought in the 1946 Free School Milk Act. She died on 6 February 1947.

bankrupted. Unemployment also affected managers, accountants and clerks employed by the firms that closed. Once such people would have been confident of finding other work but in depressed areas many found it impossible. In some places there were more than a hundred applicants for every job and many would remain unemployed until the start of the war.

A vivid picture of the devastation that bankruptcy and unemployment could bring to a family is drawn by Helen Forrester in the first part of her autobiography, *Twopence to Cross the Mersey*. After her father lost everything, through a combination of his extravagance and the Depression, her life changed forever. Born to a family with a nanny and servants and educated in a private school, she found herself, at the age of 11½, near to starvation, living in a bug-ridden slum in Liverpool and reduced to the status of a household drudge. Part of her family's problems stemmed from the fact that both her parents were extravagant by nature and neither knew how to cope in such circumstances. Her father, unable to get a job in spite of his public school education, received 43s. (£2.15) a week from the public assistance to keep his family of seven children. Her parents could not cope; her mother was used to spending more than their weekly allowance on a hat. It was to be two years before her father found work and then it was only as a poorly paid clerk.

As the oldest daughter, Helen was kept out of school to care for the family while her mother attempted to supplement the family income by taking a variety of casual jobs. Like many other women in their neighbourhood, her mother did not declare her earnings to the authorities. If she had, whatever she had earned would have been deducted from their public assistance allowance, making the exercise pointless. The extra earnings could make a large difference to the amount of food a family could buy. For the poorest, shops often split packets and sold the contents in tiny portions. Helen often bought jam by the teaspoon or a quarter of a packet of margarine. Though this put food within reach of the family when they had very little money left, it did make the cost per pound extremely high.

An interesting feature of Helen's autobiography is how little life had changed for the poorest women since Victorian times. The hunger, the dirty and ragged clothes, the overcrowding, the filth and the stench are all familiar from Dickens. While the workhouse was now used only as a last resort and limited public assistance was given to families, many still relied on the pawnbroker and charity to tide them over the worst times. The burden of keeping her family clothed and fed taxed a woman's ingenuity. Nothing was wasted. A fire could be kept burning with rubbish collected from the streets. Jumpers, scarves and gloves could be provided for a few pence by buying a pile of woollens that were beyond repair, unravelling them and using the wool to knit new clothes.

'Amy Wonderful Amy' Johnson (1903–1941)

In 1930, Amy Johnson became the first woman to fly solo from England to Australia when she landed Jason, her tiny Gypsy Moth, in Darwin on 24 May. The journey had taken her 19½ days, just 4 days short of the record. It was a great achievement for someone who had been flying little over a year and who had been told after her first lesson to give up. During the flight, she broke the record to Karachi by two days and, had she not had a number of problems with her aeroplane on route, she might well have broken the record to Australia. Her achievement inspired a number of songs including 'Amy' with its refrain, 'Amy Wonderful Amy', 'The Lone Dove' and 'Call me Johnnie', the last a reference to Amy's nickname.

Her early life made her an unlikely candidate for such an achievement. In the 1920s most

women flyers came from wealthy, aristocratic backgrounds. Amy was born in Hull, Yorkshire, on 1 July 1903 to a middle class family. She went to Sheffield University in 1923, where she graduated in economics. After her degree she moved to London where she worked as a secretary to a solicitor. She became interested in flying and joined the London Aeroplane Club, paying for her early lessons from her salary. Later, when she gave up her job and took up flying seriously, she borrowed money from her father. When she decided to make the record attempt, he was unable to meet the full costs and she was forced to seek sponsorship.

In 1929 she gained her pilot's certificate. She was not a natural flyer, but she made up for it with her sheer determination and courage. Soon after, she became the first woman to qualify as an aircraft ground engineer. Her interest in mechanics was unusual among women pilots but it stood her in good stead during her record-breaking flights. On several occasions her engineering knowledge enabled her to rectify bodged jobs done by some of the enthusiastic but less knowledgeable mechanics who came to her assistance on route.

In July 1932, she married the famous aviator Jim Mollison who held the record for the solo flight from England to Capetown. In November of that year, clearly not content to be a stay at home wife, she set off on an attempt to break his record. She succeeded by completing the journey in 4 days and 7 hours, beating his record by over 10 hours. She surprised many people, including her husband, who thought that she would not have the stamina to endure such a long flight. She flew back, setting another record in the process. She continued to make long distance flights both with her husband and on her own, though her marriage did not last long and she was divorced in 1938.

When war broke out Amy joined the Air Transport Authority flying aircraft from the factories to airfields. Although she was one of the more experienced pilots in the ATA, when she joined she had to start at the bottom and take simple tests before she was allowed to fly. She was soon promoted and transported planes across the country.

On a routine flight on 5 January 1941, she crashed into the Thames estuary towards the end of a flight from Prestwick, in Scotland, to Kidlington. Her body was never found. The cause of her crash was a mystery and there were conflicting reports about what happened.

David Luff, in his recent biography, *Amy Johnson: Enigma in the Sky*, suggests that she was shot down by anti-aircraft fire after nervous gunners failed to recognise her plane. She was not expected in the area as she was well off course when the accident happened. He points to inconsistencies in the witness statements and implies that the authorities covered up the accident rather than admit that they had shot down a national heroine. In support of his theory he points to the fact that parts of her crashed plane were quietly disposed of – an unusual decision given her status. There was never an official enquiry and there has never been any attempt to salvage her aircraft even though it lies in shallow water.

During the 1930s many poor women struggled to bring up a family in rented rooms which were often extremely difficult to keep clean. In 1930 only a third of homes had electricity so most houses were lit by gas. Many older houses had outdoor lavatories and no bathrooms. In some areas, lavatories had to be shared by several families. Hot water was heated on a fire or stove, which was difficult where cooking facilities were shared. Helen Forrester recalls the dismay her mother felt when the family was given a turkey one Christmas. Although they desperately needed food, they had no oven in their rented rooms and they cooked their meagre meals on an open fire. It looked as though they would not be able to use the turkey, until a neighbour came to the rescue and cooked it in the ancient oven attached to the fireplace in her room.

Home sweet home – life in suburbia

In sharp contrast to the Depression-hit areas, standards of living were rising in the more prosperous parts of the country. New homes, away from city centres, were being built by local authorities and by private developers. Women from the better-off working class families who were able to afford the higher rents of the new homes found themselves living in houses or flats with inside lavatories, bathrooms and hot running water. For those who had lived in overcrowded rented rooms in the inner cities, life in their new homes must have seemed like heaven. Even those who moved from relatively comfortable properties in the towns and cities would have been delighted with the luxury of electricity and hot water. With the move, a woman's life became more comfortable and caring for a home less strenuous.

For those who could afford them, the houses advertised by the private developers offered a new life as well as a new home. Leafy tree-lined streets promised quiet, genteel comfort away from the hustle and bustle of the towns and cities. Gardens were a feature of the new houses and gardening became a hobby. In London, the suburbs so lovingly eulogised by John Betjeman followed the underground out to places as distant as Ruislip, Morden and Mill Hill. Husbands were able to leave their mock Tudor homes in semi-rural avenues and be in their city offices within an hour. Meanwhile their wives stayed at home to polish their furniture and tend their neat gardens.

While a move to the suburbs promised a near paradise, it was not long before some found that the reality was not quite as rosy as painted in the advertisements. A growing sense of isolation created problems for many women. While it was true that their new homes were more comfortable and easier to clean, many working class women missed the extended families and support systems of their tight knit communities. Middle class women were also affected. In many cases professional women, who had left their jobs when they married, found themselves bored and lonely. The suburbs were bereft of art galleries, concert halls and cinemas. Worse still, middle class women who in the past would have had at least one maid of all work found themselves forced to do their own housework, sometimes with the help of a 'daily', as the shortage of servants became acute.

In some cases their load was lightened by the new labour-saving devices such as vacuum cleaners and washing machines. Yet it was these same devices that were, in part, the cause of the servant shortage. In more prosperous areas the new light industries were tempting women away from domestic service. Work on the assembly line in places like the Hoover factory in Perivale, West London, was dull and repetitive but it offered regular hours and higher wages than domestic service. When offered an alternative, few women would consider a job as a live-in domestic.

The shortage of servants encouraged the wealthy to move to smaller homes where fewer servants were needed. For others, the new domestic appliances helped to alleviate the loss of a maid. The number of homes with electricity increased throughout the decade, and by the end of the 1930s only a third of homes were without it. As a result more women were able to enjoy the benefits of the new electrical appliances. Ironing was made easier as electric irons replaced the old heavy flat irons, but only the well off could afford vacuum cleaners and even fewer had washing machines. Although the new houses were easier to clean, women were encouraged by advertisements and magazines to raise their standards of cleanliness. As a result, many spent hours striving to achieve the spotless house. At the same time that married women were being discouraged from working they were being persuaded that caring for their homes was a worthwhile substitute.

The move to new, easier to manage homes, combined with a fall in the size in their families, should have given women a more relaxed life. But the lack of stimulation, the loneliness and the pressure to have the perfect home had the reverse effect and led to what the medical profession termed 'suburban neurosis'. Their answer to this new phenomenon was to advise women to find a new interest: the suggestions offered ranged from taking up dressmaking to having another baby. There was no acceptance that, in order to stay sane, some women needed more than a life of 'domestic bliss'. Many women turned to the Townswomen's Guilds (see box, p. 80) for company and some stimulation. But here, too, much of the emphasis, at least at local level during the 1930s, was on homemaking and traditional crafts.

Equality vs special treatment

Although the 1930s are sometimes seen as a quiet period in the advancement of women's rights, the campaign continued but with a shift in emphasis. The sense of urgency that had characterised earlier campaigns died down once women finally won the vote on the same terms as men. As far as some women were concerned the battle had been won, while others believed that the vote was just one step on the road to equality. After 1928, women no longer had a common goal and campaigning on women's issues took different directions.

The main differences of opinion lay in the way that campaigners viewed a woman's role. Those who fought for equality wanted no concessions made towards women. They objected to protective legislation, feeling that it undermined the struggle for equality. These women wanted equal pay and equal opportunities in education and work. They wanted the end of the marriage bar and saw no reason for women to stop work even after they had children. To the many upper and upper middle class women who took this stance the idea of working mothers was not a radical one for most of them were accustomed to the idea of leaving children in the care of their nannies.

Some women objected to the glorification of homebound motherhood and rebelled against the idea that they belonged in the home. The writer and close friend of Vera Brittain, Winifred Holtby, whose own mother was an alderman, argued in favour of working mothers or at least mothers with interests outside the home. She claimed that a mother who had her own interests and experience of the world was in a better position to guide her children, especially when they were ready to go out into the world. She was also scathing about homemaking, considering it to be a narrow and unfulfilling occupation.

In the 1930s those in favour of equality had a hard time of it. During the harsh economic climate of the Depression, the majority of women were not interested in the marriage bar or in equal pay. They were more concerned about their husband's jobs. Some even blamed women for male unemployment, though the greatest unemployment was found in the traditional male industries. A further blow to the cause of equality came in the Anomalies Act of 1931, which prevented a large number of married women from receiving unemployment benefit, even though they had paid their contributions. It is ironic that this blow was dealt by Margaret Bondfield, the Minister of Labour at the time and the first woman to become a cabinet minister.

The main reason given for refusing women equal pay was that men needed more money because they had families to support. This argument, accepted by many women at the time, ignored the fact that men without families also earned more than women did. It assumed that women had no dependants, forgetting the widows with children and the single women who supported their elderly parents. There was no call for these women to be paid a family wage.

Eleanor Rathbone, who became an MP in 1929, had very definite views about the way forward for women. She believed that women had special needs and that, rather than trying to treat women as the equals of men, their differences should be recognised and catered for. She believed that the majority of women were happiest being wives and mothers and they should be encouraged to stay at home. Although her views sound remarkably like those of the Victorians she differed from them in the value that she placed on a woman's role. In her view, homemakers and mothers played such a vital role in society that their efforts should be acknowledged and rewarded by the state. She believed there should be no 'family wage'. In her vision of society, all people would be paid as individuals, with the state supporting the family through direct

An early 1930s Empire Marketing Board poster, 'The Good Shopper'. Not only was food plentiful for the wealthy, as the advertisement indicates, but in the more prosperous parts of the country the middle and upper classes were encouraged to shop for the new electrical goods.

payments to mothers. She rejected the campaign for equal pay, insisting that mothers' allowances should come first.

Her campaign for mother's allowances began as early as 1917 after she realised that women and children who were in receipt of separation allowances were often healthier during the war than they had been before it. Most men gave their wives a set amount each week and usually kept something back for themselves even when there was not enough to feed their families. In Helen Forrester's autobiography there are references to her father having a drink and smoking even though his family often had no more than bread and margarine to eat. Although many husbands provided well for their families a minority kept their families short, preferring to spend their money in the public houses. In Eleanor Rathbone's view the best way to alleviate poverty was to reduce a woman's dependence on a man. With money going directly to mothers she believed that children and their mothers would be a great deal healthier.

Women's health

In 1933, a group of women's organisations commissioned a survey of women's health. The Women's Health Enquiry studied a cross section of married working class women. The report that followed in 1939 showed a clear link between poverty and ill health. The majority suffered from a number of minor ailments largely caused by their living conditions. Poor housing, poor diet and, in some cases, large families all contributed to their poor health. Most of these women fed their families as best they could, often going without food when it was scarce. The report showed that the staple diet of most of the women surveyed was little more than bread and margarine supplemented by copious amounts of weak tea.

Although less than a third of the women suffered from serious conditions, few could be described as fit and healthy. The majority of women suffered from a range of minor ailments including backache, indigestion, constipation, headaches and varicose veins. While these problems were not life threatening they did make it harder for women to cope and minor problems left untreated could develop into more serious illnesses. The poorer married women rarely saw a doctor unless they were seriously ill, as they were not entitled to free medical care. Few would spend precious money on a doctor's bill for a minor ailment. In many cases it was not a doctor that they needed but a better diet, fresh air and time to rest.

At the beginning of the decade, pregnancy was still a cause of health problems for women. Childbirth was still dangerous in the 1930s and mortality rates were high. Health problems could affect women of all classes. Helen Forrester's mother, while still living an affluent middle class existence, had become seriously ill after the birth of her seventh child. She had needed an operation and was very weak for a long time afterwards, though her fall into extreme poverty soon after the operation probably delayed her recovery. In 1930 the Government finally accepted the need to provide birth control advice in special cases. After years of campaigning by the birth control pioneers, a Ministry of Health circular was sent out to clinics allowing them to give birth control advice to married women whose health would be endangered by further pregnancies. Further advances were made in 1939 when the Family Planning Association was set up. By the end of the 1930s large families were no longer the norm.

The relief of having reliable birth control advice must have been tremendous. Married women no longer faced the possibility of having a child a year throughout their fertile years. While that may not have been common, it did happen to some. In the file of correspondence discussed below, someone inserted a newspaper cutting that referred to 48 children sired by 3 men. One man is quoted as saying that of all his 25 children, the youngest (who was in court on a charge) was the only one to have given him trouble. While it does not say whether the children all had the same mother, it is possible. Another example of a large family appears in *Out of the Doll's House,* where a Mr and Mrs Terry are pictured with some of their nineteen children. In the photograph, Mrs Terry looks surprisingly cheerful and robust.

Yet in spite of the benefits of birth control many were still hostile. The Roman Catholic Church opposed it and women's magazines, probably concerned with the effect on circulation, ignored it. The ease with which condoms could be obtained caused some sections of the community great concern. In the National Archives there is a file of correspondence (HO 45/17040) about the sale of condoms through automatic vending machines. It contains a letter from a Rev. Basil Wood who referred to the machines as a 'dangerous public evil'. He wrote that they had been placed outside shops for 'the sale of rubber goods for immoral purposes', and claimed that the machines provided 'a serious temptation to the young'.

The file also contains newspaper cuttings on the same subject. The reports claimed that the machines were lowering moral standards and were a 'commercial exploitation of vice'. They also condemned manufacturers for 'enriching themselves by encouraging lust in men and women'. Concern was expressed about the effects on young men and there were claims that the machines were likely to corrupt adolescent youths. The chief constable of Southport wrote that 'in one city schoolboys obtained rubber contraceptives by inserting discs in the machines'.

The file also contained objections to women being given contraceptive advice. One objector claimed that if a woman's health was at risk from further pregnancy, it was her husband's responsibility to go and speak to a doctor. He also rejected the idea that birth control would be of use to a woman married to a 'brute',

arguing that the use of birth control would merely encourage a brute to bother his wife. Pregnancy, he suggested, was the best protection from a brutish husband's 'unwelcome advances'. His real agenda, however, became apparent when he concluded that the declining birth rate 'menaces the very existence of our race'.

Birth control became more acceptable during the 1930s, but the open display of condom vending machines, like this one attached to the outside wall of a chemist's shop (right of photograph) offended many people.

The Women's League for Health and Beauty

As well as wanting to control their fertility, women in the 1930s were becoming interested in the idea of taking control of their health. In 1930 Mary Bagot Stack founded the Women's League for Health and Beauty with the aim of bringing the benefits of exercise to a wider group of women. In the following year she published *Building The Body Beautiful*. She taught that a woman could improve her health and keep doctors at bay by taking regular exercise. To further this she created a series of exercises for women. Some, which were influenced by the yoga she had learned when she was in India, were designed to improve posture. Others were a form of expressive dance and were done to music. She trained teachers in her methods and before long hundreds of classes were being held across the country.

By 1930 there were many women living in towns and cities who worked in jobs which involved little exercise, and these were the women that the Women's League for Health and Beauty was aimed at. Shop assistants, office workers and women who worked on the assembly lines in the new light industries flocked to classes which were held across the country in places as diverse as village halls and factories. As well as teaching movement and dance, the classes also involved discreet teaching on personal hygiene when appropriate.

On 3 June 1935, *The Times* reported on a performance by the Women's League for Health and Beauty, held in Olympia. The performance was impressive, with 2,500 women taking part in a series of colourful dances, tableaux and demonstrations. An interesting feature of the report is the way it indicates the attitudes towards older women at the time. It was felt necessary to report that 'sixty-four mothers and a number of grandmothers took part' and later commented on one exhibition, which was performed only by mothers, that it 'proved that in agility and energy they could compete fully with their daughters'. The 1935 performance was also a tribute to the founder who had died earlier in the year. In the finale, a symbolic torch was handed to her daughter, Phyllis Stack, who had taken over running the League.

The rumblings of war

Although women in the 1930s seemed to be concentrating on the domestic sphere, the rise of fascism in Europe brought politics firmly back into their lives. As with their male counterparts, women were divided on the position they took. Some, like Vera Brittain, maintained their pacifist stance, but others, appalled by the doctrines of fascism, argued for rearmament. A few, however, with a bewildering disregard for the attitude of fascists towards women, joined the British Union of Fascists. Political differences even occurred within families. While Unity Mitford supported Mosley, her sister Jessica, who had left-wing sympathies, went off to support the Republicans in Spain.

The hatred of fascism inspired a number of British women to join the international brigades who went to Spain to fight. The first British volunteer to be killed fighting in the war was a woman, the English artist and sculptor, Felicia Browne. Ellen Wilkinson went to Spain as an observer and argued in Parliament against the policy of non-intervention. Some went as reporters but it was rare for a newspaper to post a woman to a war zone. When Hilde Marchant was sent to

Members of the Women's
League of Health and Beauty
rehearsing for a keep fit
demonstration in Hyde Park,
1933.

Spain it was to report on the woman's angle in Madrid. Shiela [*sic*] Grant Duff,
who was once told to write about fashion when she asked for a job, became
Britain's first woman war correspondent when she was sent to Spain to report on
the treatment of Republican prisoners. She was assigned to the job instead of one
of the newspaper's better known reporters, as the task was closer to espionage. It
was felt that as a woman she would be less conspicuous.

While only a few women volunteered to fight in the Spanish Civil War a much
larger number volunteered for the International Medical Service. As in the First
World War, they went as doctors and nurses to care for the sick and wounded.
Once there they faced appalling conditions. Others went to help refugees. Leah
Manning, who later became an MP, and Edith Pye, helped to evacuate almost
4,000 children from Bilbao. It is interesting that in a file in the National Archives
(FO 371/31285) labelled 'Humanitarian aid to Spain', no mention is made of the
work of these women. Instead the file simply gives statistics on the number of
refugees removed from Spanish ports.

War and the threat of it overshadowed the lives of women in the second half of the decade. Lessons learned from the bombing of Spanish cities led to the formation of the Air Raid Warden service in 1937. By 1938 many people, women included, had joined the service. The tension created by the threat of war was

The Townswomen's Guilds

In 1928 leading suffragists of the National Union of Societies for Equal Citizenship formed the Townswomen's Guilds (TG) to educate ordinary women in their new political role as voters. As the movement grew it developed to reflect the interests of its members, most of whom were housewives. In 1932 the TG became an independent organisation and in the following year launched the *Townswoman*. Although it dropped the emphasis on politics it continued with its aim of educating ordinary women. Local guilds held debates and meetings with speakers who discussed a wide range of topics. Members learned to speak in public and sit on committees. The local groups also provided support for women and gave them a chance to meet and socialise.

The TG continued to spread in the 1930s and by the start of the Second World War was in a position to offer valuable assistance to the war effort. Among their activities were helping with the evacuation of children, providing canteens, knitting and raising funds. By 1953 the TG felt confident enough to become a campaigning organisation. It began with an anti-litter campaign and continued to show an interest in the environment with a 'Going for green' campaign. It has also campaigned on the issue of women's health, putting pressure on the Government to improve facilities for cervical screening. Members of individual guilds wrote to MPs, health authorities and hospitals in support of the campaign. The TG continues to campaign on women's health.

Although some tend to scoff at the TG, seeing it as an out-dated and reactionary organisation, it has never been afraid to embrace controversial issues. In the 1960s it campaigned for improved sex education in schools and more recently it has actively campaigned in favour of the legalisation of cannabis for medical use. Over the years it has acted as a pressure group opposing GM foods and the use of growth hormones designed to increase the milk yield in dairy cows.

The TG works both at national and local level. The individual guilds hold local meetings and deal with local issues though they also join in the national campaigns. Fund-raising for both local and national causes is well supported. The Child Nutrition Unit in Dakar was made possible by money raised by the TG. The original aim of education has not been forgotten. Although the majority of its members are over 60 they are very much concerned with current issues including topics as diverse as IT and understanding the Euro. The TG has IT schools and holds Women in Europe conferences.

recorded in the work of Mass-Observation organisation, which was set up in 1937 to record life in Britain. *Wartime Women: A Mass-Observation Anthology*, edited by Dorothy Sheridan, contains extracts from the record of the daily lives, the thoughts and feelings of a cross section of women between the years 1937 and 1945. In one extract, Miss Pringle, a young Liverpool teacher, records how she became involved with the Air Raid Precautions (ARP) in 1938, when her school became a centre for the distribution of gas masks. She wrote about the need to reassure the children while they were being fitted with the masks. On the whole they were successful and only a few were frightened by the experience. Some children, not recognising the smell of disinfectant used on the masks, were convinced that the masks were filled with gas.

Others were also preparing for war. On 16 October 1937, *The Times* reported on an initiative by the Council for Emergency Service to train women for future roles as officers in the women's services should war break out. The system used for their training was similar to that used by the Officers Training Corps (OTC) which had prepared many a public schoolboy for his role in the First World War. Vera Brittain's brother and his close friends, all of whom were killed in the First World War, had belonged to the OTC.

Experienced officers of the Army and Air Force, obviously with the blessing of the War Office and Air Ministry, trained the women, although neither government department was directly involved in recruiting them. The women were all volunteers and it is interesting to note, given the continued existence of the marriage bar, that married women were included in the training schemes. *The Times* was quick to point out that the married women had made arrangements for the care of their families in case they were needed and had obtained their husband's approval for their actions. It was a foretaste of things to come.

What did you do in the war, mummy?

The life that I have is all that I have, and the life that I have is yours

FROM THE POEM CODE BY LEO MARKS THAT WAS USED BY VIOLETTE SZABO

For children growing up in a city like Portsmouth in the late 1940s and early 1950s there was no escaping the Second World War, even though we were too young to remember it. It was all around us; evident in the bombsites we played on and in our homes, overcrowded with bombed-out relatives waiting for their promised new houses. We knew about the bombs, we knew about Hitler and we knew about pilots, soldiers and sailors. But we never knew what our mothers did.

We had no idea that many of them had worn uniforms, that some had operated anti-aircraft guns and that others had driven trucks. We knew nothing of their work as lumberjacks or in intelligence and even when we were old enough for history lessons we were never taught anything about the part they played. Years later the programme *Dads' Army* reinforced this ignorance; the only women who appeared were housewives anxious to get their 'rations'. Yet without the work of its women during the war, it is difficult to see how Britain would have survived.

When war broke out its immediate effect was to increase women's unemployment. Six months into the war, however, it became clear that women would have to be recruited in large numbers. They were needed in factories, on the land, in hospitals, and in offices. The armed forces needed them to release men for the front and they were needed by the civil defence organisations. The Government appealed to women to volunteer for war work but the appeal met with limited success. A Mass-Observation (M-O) report in March 1941, which is included in Dorothy Sheridan's anthology (see p. 81), criticised the way the Government and the press handled the campaign to recruit volunteers, blaming its lack of success on poor preparation and the lack of information available. Women MPs were also critical, claiming that if the Government would provide nurseries and give detailed information about the working conditions and rates of pay on offer, women would volunteer in their thousands.

By 1941 the shortage of labour was so acute that drastic action was needed. In March all women aged between 19 and 40 had to register at their local labour exchange where they were allocated to essential work. Even this was not enough and in December 1941 Britain became the only country to conscript women. Women aged between 20 and 30 were called up and most were sent to join the ATS or to work in the munitions factories. Women with children under 14 were exempt, as were women who were caring for a number of essential workers. Single women without dependants were considered to be mobile and could be sent anywhere to work.

Married women, however, were always found work in their locality. Many returned to jobs they had before the war but, as they were regarded as being temporary, they were often paid less than when they were single. Even though married women were being asked to work, the marriage bar continued in some professions. Some civil servants, for example, were allowed to remain in their jobs when they married but had to resign first and be re-classified as temporary staff. The conscription of women was unpopular with many men, who objected to their wives and daughters being forced into war work while they were away. The M-O report referred to above quoted a soldier who wrote to the *Daily Sketch* objecting to the conscription of women. He claimed that the very reason that he and others like him were fighting was to protect 'our wives and sweethearts'.

Objections from men caused the Government some concern, as fathers, husbands and fiancés were used to making decisions for women. One woman's father refused to let her volunteer to drive an ambulance and she was forced to choose alternative work. A wartime advertisement for Rinso soap powder shows the attitudes of the time. Entitled 'Her husband had doubts', it told the story in a

OPPOSITE
A member of the WRNS makes fast the motor boat used to ferry mail and goods to ships at anchor, 1942.

strip cartoon of a woman whose husband felt that a part-time job was too much for her. She agreed with him until a friend advised her to use Rinso, which cut the time it took to do the weekly wash. The cartoon ended with a contented husband praising his wife for managing to run the house and work part time – this on a washday and thanks to Rinso of course.

Fathers and husbands were not the only ones who needed persuading to accept women in the workplace. Women's work in the factories was crucial but, as in the First World War, many employers were not convinced that they were capable of doing 'a man's job'. To help overcome this prejudice, the Ministry of Labour and National Service published a book called *Women in Engineering*. The book, a copy of which is in the National Archives (LAB 44/252), contains photographs showing women doing a range of skilled jobs and using a variety of machines. The book was issued to technical officers, labour supply inspectors and exchange managers to help them convince employers that women were capable of skilled work.

Women in the auxiliary forces

As in the previous war, women were recruited to release men for the front. In most cases, whether they joined the WAAF (Women's Auxiliary Air Force), WRNS (Women's Royal Naval Service) or ATS (Auxiliary Territorial Service), the work they did was similar to the work they had done before the war. Some transferred their office skills and worked in administration as secretaries, shorthand typists and clerks, while others took on the more domestic roles of cooks, waitresses and cleaners. For women not employed in traditional roles, the services provided training. Driving was an important skill and women were employed as drivers in each of the services. Many of the women who drove in the 1940s and the 1950s, including the present Queen, were taught to drive in the services.

As the war progressed, women took over highly specialised tasks unlike anything they had done in civilian life. They worked as visual signallers, flight engineers and radar plotters. They debriefed aircrews and worked in intelligence. They operated searchlights and anti-aircraft batteries, where they did everything short of actually firing the guns. ATS mechanics could repair anything from a car to a three ton truck; the WAAF repaired aeroplanes; and WRNS repaired ships. An advertisement for the WAAF, in which a pilot boasts that 'Joan's doing a real job now', called for women to apply to be balloon operators, meteorologists and radio operators as well as the more traditional nursing orderlies and administrators. Women in the WRNS worked on harbour craft and were involved in the dangerous job of coastal mine spotting. It seemed that women could do almost

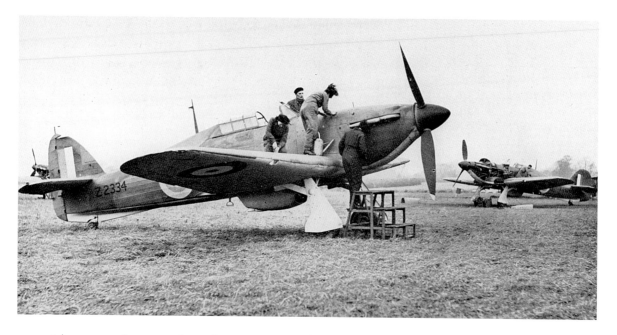

Women flight engineers preparing aircraft, 1942.

every job except take on combat roles, go to sea on HMS ships or fly with the RAF.

While the first two objections are understandable in the context of the period, it is more difficult, given the high profile of women aviators in the 1930s, to understand why the WAAF did not train or use women pilots. As Amy Johnson (see also p. 70) discovered, if a woman wanted a job flying during the war she had to join the civilian Air Transport Auxiliary (ATA) where her flying duties were confined to ferrying planes between airfields. Intrepid women flyers like Amy were not allowed to undertake the taxing missions more suited to their temperament and skills. It is ironic that while several of the Special Operations Executive's (SOE) women secret agents (see p. 88) were given commissions in the WAAF, their fellow officers were not allowed to fly them to their destinations. While it is true that flying personnel and supplies to help the resistance was dangerous work, male pilots were parachuting women agents into France where, if caught, they faced almost certain death.

The most popular services were the WAAF and the WRNS (nicknamed Wrens) and they had little problem with recruiting as both had a glamorous image due, in part, to the colour and cut of their uniforms. But while many women were happy to sign on, not all men were keen on their wives and sweethearts joining the services. When 18-year-old Betty Turner (later Storey; see also pp. 91, 97, 107) wanted to join the WRNS, as her mother had done during the First World War, she found that the men in her life did not approve. She thought that she might have been able to persuade her father, but her fiancé was set against it. As they lived close to Portsmouth, he was no doubt aware of the sailors' adage 'Up with the lark, to bed with a Wren'.

The worries that service life would corrupt a girl came, in part, from the belief that immorality was rife in the women's auxiliary forces. Rumours that women were leaving the services in droves because of pregnancy and venereal disease swept through Britain during the early part of the war. These rumours were so widespread that an investigating committee was formed: it not only found that the rumours were unjustified, but that women in the forces had a lower incidence of pregnancy and disease than in the civilian population.

The ATS was the least popular of the services and conscription was needed to make up the numbers required. This was partly due to its unflattering uniform, a fact recognised by magazines which advised their readers on the best shade of lipstick to wear with khaki. Attempts were made to sell the ATS as a glamorous service but Eleanor Rathbone MP objected in Parliament to this approach, claiming intelligent women would not respond to such appeals. She was not alone in her objections and one recruitment poster was banned for being too frivolous. A late boost for recruitment came in 1945 when the young Princess Elizabeth, against the wishes of her parents and the Government, joined the ATS and trained as a driver and mechanic.

The Princess Elizabeth in her ATS uniform, 1945.

A different reason for the unpopularity of the ATS was put forward by Mrs Trowbridge, whose diary extract is in *Wartime Women*. While she conceded that the colour of their stockings put some girls off, she claimed that the real reason for girls not joining was the patronising and arrogant attitudes of the ATS officers. According to Mrs Trowbridge, ATS officers assumed that any girl with a northern accent was uneducated 'and proceed to treat her as if she were a kitchenmaid being interviewed by an ill-bred duchess'.

West Indian women volunteers

Although there was a shortage of women in the ATS there was a group of women whose services were not welcome. A large file of correspondence in the National Archives (CO 323/1863/24) deals with the recruitment of women from the West Indies for service in the UK. It includes discussion on whether the War Office should be allowed to limit its recruitment in the West Indies to white women. The topic sparked a great deal of heated discussion when the Colonial Office discovered the War Office's intention of recruiting white West Indian women for the ATS for service in Washington.

The Colonial Office objected to what it saw as the War Office's colour prejudice and demanded a reason for its attitude. The Colonial Office was also angered by the Army's treatment of Miss Curtis, a girl from Bermuda, who had been provisionally accepted for the ATS but was rejected when they discovered that she was not white. The Colonial Office spent a great deal of time and effort trying to get Miss Curtis accepted by the Army. Eventually, in a weary compromise, the War Office was allowed to recruit white women from the West Indies for service in the United States on condition that they also recruited a small group of black women. Miss Curtis was accepted into this group even though women from Bermuda were not included in the scheme.

The correspondence shows that it was not only women who wished to join the ATS who were rejected. In 1943 fifty partially trained nurses from the Newill Nuttal Hospital in Jamaica offered their services to the UK. They were rejected. The excuse given to the Governor of Jamaica was that it was not viable to take untrained nurses from Jamaica because of the shortage of shipping. The Governor was told that fully trained personnel were still wanted but added the details of any volunteers should include 'whether applicants are white or coloured'.

In spite of the demand for women workers in the UK, the Ministry of Labour was 'not at all anxious to import women from the West Indies for war work in view of the social and other difficulties'. As the Ministry knew that recruitment could not be restricted to white women they were reluctant to take any women from the

West Indies. It wrote, however, that it was concerned not to hurt the feelings of women who might want to volunteer and offered 'hope of employment' to fully qualified women. A note in the margin added that 'this condition would probably rule out most coloured women'.

The file (CO 968/81/5) shows that the Air Ministry was also reluctant to recruit women from the West Indies. They claimed, in correspondence with the Governor of Bermuda, that entry to the WAAF was extremely limited, even in the UK, and that they were only recruiting for three or four highly specialised trades. They agreed, however, to consider individual applications from women with a practical or mechanical aptitude who were of good character, intelligent and able to take on responsibility. Some women were not put off by the requirements and the WAAF took on approximately 80 women from the West Indies to serve in Britain.

The WAAF also enlisted girls from ethnic minorities who were based in the UK, as the case of Lilian Bader shows. Lilian, whose story is in the Imperial War Museum's *Together* education pack, was a mixed race orphan who, like all the girls in her orphanage, had been trained as a domestic. During the war she responded to the call for girls to work for the Navy, Army and Air Force Institutes (NAAFI). Although some concern was shown regarding her colour at her interview, they took her on, but she was dismissed after seven weeks on the orders of Head Office.

She made several unsuccessful applications to rejoin the NAAFI, then reluctantly returned to domestic service. When she heard that the WAAF had enlisted women from the West Indies she applied to join and was accepted. Although she started by working as a domestic she took a course to become an Instrument Repairer which she passed 'First Class'. Some time after becoming a Leading Aircraftwoman she was promoted to Acting Corporal.

Women agents and the Resistance

The most difficult of all services to get into, as it was by invitation only, was the highly secret Special Operations Executive (SOE). The SOE was formed to work with the Resistance to create havoc behind enemy lines, and it employed women from the start. It recruited women who were fluent in a foreign language, trained them as special agents and then parachuted them into enemy territory. Recruits were often civilians but once they joined SOE they were usually assigned to either the First Aid Nursing Yeomanry (FANY) or the WAAF.

The SOE recruited about three thousand women but they did not all work directly in the field. Many of the women were very young and some, like Violette Szabo (see profile) were mothers. Fifty women were parachuted into France where

Violette Szabo (1921–1945)

In 1946, a year after she was executed by the Gestapo in the notorious Ravensbruck Concentration Camp, Violette Szabo was awarded the George Cross for her bravery under torture. Although other women met her fate, her story is one of the most familiar thanks to the 1958 film *Carve her Name with Pride* starring Virginia McKenna. She was only 23 when she was executed.

Like many agents, Violette had lived in France during her childhood. She was born in Paris in 1921 to a French mother and English father. She came to England while still a child and lived in London. She was a tomboy and a daredevil who loved to challenge her brother. This aspect of her personality was noted during her training with the SOE. When she was nineteen, she married Etienne Szabo, a captain in the French Foreign Legion. He was killed at El Alamein and never saw his daughter Tania. Violette's anger at his death was a motivating factor in her decision to join the SOE.

Although she was the mother of a young child, the SOE recruited her as an agent in 1943 and gave her a commission in the FANYs. During her training, she proved to be an excellent shot and was one of the most physically capable

A cutting from a newspaper dated 30 March 1946 reporting on Violette Szabo's heroism.

women. Within a few months she was sent to France where she successfully completed her mission and returned to England. She was parachuted back into France immediately after the Normandy landings, but unknown to HQ she and her group had been betrayed.

In the events leading up to her capture, Violette refused the chance to escape, choosing instead to stay with her colleague and fight. Marcus Binney, in *Women Who Lived for Danger*, claims that, although she did not have the blazing gun battle portrayed in the film, her courage was even more remarkable. While retreating from the Germans she became too exhausted to continue. She persuaded her colleague to go on without her while she stayed and held up the Germans. She only surrendered when she ran out of ammunition. A witness reported that he heard firing for over half an hour, which shows a remarkable coolness on her part. As she only had sixty-four rounds of ammunition when she started she must have conserved her ammunition in order to give her colleague as much time as possible to escape.

Although the George Cross is the highest civilian honour, Dame Irene Ward MP believed that Violette should have been awarded the Victoria Cross, a military medal. In correspondence in a file in the National Archives (WO 32/20708), Dame Irene argued that Violette's actions in resisting capture entitled her to a military medal. Dame Irene was convinced that the only reason that Violette was not awarded the Victoria Cross was because she was a woman. The Government argued that she had been decorated for her bravery under torture and therefore the George Cross was appropriate. They refused to accept Dame Irene's arguments but the fact remains that Violette was involved in military action before her capture; holding off the enemy by firing a sten gun was hardly a civilian pursuit.

they worked as couriers and wireless operators; some were also involved in sabotage and spying. Their work was extremely dangerous as the Germans showed no mercy to women agents. Fifteen of the fifty women parachuted into France were captured and of those twelve were executed, Violette Szabo among them.

Most of the agents had a rigorous training before they were parachuted into enemy-held territory. As well as being given cover stories and tested on how well they knew them, they were taught how to parachute out of an aircraft. Many were trained as wireless operators and some were taught to use explosives. Although British women were officially banned from combat roles, the women of the SOE were trained alongside men in hand to hand combat and in the use of weapons. Violette Szabo was to put her training to good use in the events leading up to her capture.

This aspect of their training was not always appreciated by the men in charge of the groups they joined in the field. One group leader wrote to complain that although one of his operatives, Paddy O'Sullivan, had spent six weeks in Scotland being trained in combat and the use of explosives, no one had thought to ensure she could ride a bicycle. In France the bicycle was the most common and least suspicious form of transport and women couriers could cycle hundreds of kilometres in a week. Paddy had to learn to ride but her lessons on public roads in France broke one of the most important rules of the SOE, not to attract attention.

A file in the National Archives (KV 4/172), containing notes of a SOE training course, stressed the importance of keeping a low profile at all times. The course gave advice on avoiding detection and, indirectly, gave an insight into some of the different habits of the French and English. As well pointing out the different ways to use cutlery, agents were reminded to remove tobacco stains from their fingers, as the tobacco in French cigarettes did not stain. As cigarettes were very difficult to obtain in France agents were also told to stop smoking. Even more intriguing was the reminder that the simple and automatic action of tucking a handkerchief into a sleeve would betray an agent, as it was known to be an English habit.

The civilian services

Life back home was a far cry from the cloak and dagger lives of the secret agents, yet it was a far from easy or safe option. At the height of the blitz women were at risk simply by going about their daily business and tens of thousands were killed in the bombing raids. They were also at risk while undertaking civil defence duties. Although they could not join the Home Guard because they were not allowed to bear arms, they became Air Raid Precaution (ARP) wardens, staffed First Aid Posts, and joined the Police Reserve and the Auxiliary Fire Service (AFS). These services, though not attracting much attention in popular histories, were an essential part of Britain's civil defences.

When Betty Turner, a shorthand typist in a Portsmouth office, registered for war work in 1941, she was offered a choice of the AFS or the Police Reserve. Although she would have preferred a job that allowed her to travel, her father refused to sign documents giving his permission, so instead she joined the AFS. Much of the work she did for the AFS was similar to work she had done before. She was still a shorthand typist and, apart from the times she was on standby, she worked from nine to five. The biggest difference in her work was that as a member of the AFS she wore a uniform and had to do drill and PE (see photograph on p. 92).

Another difference was that she was sometimes sent out in the radio car that accompanied the fire engines during air raids. When she was on standby she spent

JUST A GOOD AFTERNOON'S WORK

A Ministry of Information poster designed to persuade women who were not required to register for war work to take a part-time job. It gives some idea of how important women's work was to the war effort.

Betty Turner (centre) exercising with her Auxiliary Fire Service colleagues. Note the influence of the Women's League for Health and Beauty (see photograph on p. 79) on their movements.

the night in staff accommodation close to the fire station, but the rest of the time she lived with her parents. Betty insisted that there was nothing special or glamorous in the work she did, but the AFS was an important part of the civil defence organisation, especially in towns like Portsmouth which were regularly bombed.

The attack on the civilian population also increased the need for nurses. Not only were nurses employed in hospitals and by the services, as in the last war, but they were also needed to deal with the casualties of the bombing raids. Amy Briggs, whose diary extract is in *Wartime Women*, was a nurse who did shifts at a first aid post even though she had two young children at home. When she had finished a shift she could still be recalled to work by the sound of the air-raid siren. On 22 October 1941, she had to leave her children and return to the post at 8.30 p.m.

even though she had already worked a shift that day. As there were no bombs that night, she was able to return home after the 'all clear' at 11.32 p.m.

Another essential service was the Women's Voluntary Service (WVS), which was set up to co-ordinate the work of the women's voluntary groups. Once established the Government left them to liaise with local authorities in matters of welfare. In fact the WVS was largely responsible for dealing with the evacuation as well as the many people made homeless by the bombing. The Government also called on the WVS to distribute the 45 million ration books. While leaders of the WVS tended to be formidable upper class women, the majority of its members were usually middle-aged, middle class housewives who, although not required to do war work, nonetheless volunteered 'to do their bit' with the WVS.

The cosy image of the WVS dispensing tea and sympathy belies the extent and value of their work. They were often the first at the scene of a bombing raid, where, in a matter of minutes, they could set up an incident inquiry point to co-ordinate information for the rescue services. They organised mobile feeding stations and, for those made homeless by the raids, provided shelter at rest centres until alternative accommodation could be found. A Mass-Observation report on morale in a number of bombed cities, published in November 1940, commented favourably on the work of the WVS in keeping up morale. The report, a copy of which is in the National Archives (HO 199/442), also praised the foresight of the Coventry WVS in placing its rest centres on the periphery of the city, and recommended that the civil defence scheme followed suit.

By the end of 1941 a million women had joined the WVS. From the start, they had helped organise the mass evacuation and many took evacuees into their homes. Others had soldiers billeted on them and many knitted and darned socks for the forces. They ran canteens and they spent hours making camouflage nets. They provided nursing auxiliaries and helped with hospital services. They were active in the 'make do and mend' campaign and boosted food production by growing and preserving food. They did fire watch duties, ran advice centres and organised the collection of scarce materials, including a mountain of aluminium pots and pans. It is little wonder that this army of volunteers was sometimes referred to as the 'Fourth Service'.

Another important civilian service, despite its name, was the Women's Land Army. As in the previous war it was not a popular choice: the pay was low, the work physically demanding and the hours long. In spite of this more than 80,000 women had joined the service by 1943. The 'land girls', as they were known, worked in market gardens as well as on farms and, provided the gardens were turned over to food production, they could be employed as private gardeners. Such was the importance of the Women's Land Army to food production that it remained in

Calling all mothers

The right food and good eating habits lay the foundation of health and happiness

THE CHIEF FACTS to remember in feeding children of any age are that, in proportion to their size, children need more of the body-building foods (milk, meat, fish, cheese and eggs, dried milk and dried eggs) than do adults: And to gain their fair chance in life children *must* have their full rations and allowances. So no giving part of their meat and cheese, for instance, to grown-ups, and no putting their priority milk into the family tea-cups!

Use nearly all the Points coupons in the children's books for foods of body-building and protective value: tinned milk, meats, and fish, peas and beans, dried fruits (including prunes), etc. And—this is equally important—make sure the children have a good helping of green vegetables, either raw in salads or lightly cooked, every day.

FREE LEAFLETS. There is a series of leaflets—just published—which tell the "why's" and "how's" of planning meals for children from 1 to 17 years of age. The leaflets contain recipes as well as many useful hints. Why not send a postcard for those of interest to you? Please ask for "*How to plan meals for Children,*" and be sure to give the ages of your children. Address: Ministry of Food, (Dept 625L,) Food Advice Division, London, W.1.

Do you know . . .

Orange juice alternatives: What to give instead of orange juice when children are no longer on the Green Ration Book.

What to use for sweetening when sugar is short?

How to classify foods making menu-planning easier?

How to introduce good feeding habits without tears?

How to make delicious and nourishing mock cream?

These are just a few of the subjects covered in the "How to plan meals for Children" leaflets. See free offer in paragraph above.

An extra for young workers up to 18: It is National Milk Cocoa: a grand food and a most delicious drink. Supplies are limited, so for the time being, at any rate, National Milk Cocoa is available only to young people up to 18 years of age, and at their place of work. If your young people are not getting National Milk Cocoa please urge them to ask about it. It is so important for them, and so nice.

ISSUED BY THE MINISTRY OF FOOD   (S92)

existence until well after the end of war and was not disbanded until 1950.

Women were also recruited into the Timber Corps where they felled trees and ran sawmills. Most people found it difficult to believe that women could do the physically demanding and highly skilled work of lumberjacks. But, as in so many other areas in the workplace, when they were given the opportunity and the training to do a man's job, women proved that they could do it and do it well.

They also serve – women in traditional roles

Although more than seven million women were involved in paid war work, more than eight million were classified as full-time housewives. The description is misleading, as it suggests that they did little to help the war effort. Yet the full-time housewife was the mainstay of voluntary groups such as the WVS, and even those who did not join any of the voluntary services played their part in the war effort. The importance of their work was recognised by the Government, which exempted women who cared for essential workers from call-up. As well as caring for their families, many housewives made informal arrangements to look after children or to help with the shopping for women who went out to work.

In wartime conditions being a housewife was far from easy. Food shortages and the subsequent long queues turned the simple task of providing a meal for a family into a feat of endurance. The Ministry of Food and the Ministry of Agriculture bombarded women with advice, and magazines were recruited to help get the message across. Food rationing meant that meals required careful planning, but plans could come to nothing if, after hours of queuing, the grocer or butcher had run out of an essential ingredient. Women had to learn to adapt and prepare meals with whatever ingredients were available, while eking out their family's rations.

Food was available on the black market, but it was expensive and few could afford to buy it regularly. Instead, women used a variety of substitute foods. Ingenious recipes were dreamt up using the plentiful carrots and potatoes, and the word 'mock' in front of familiar dishes became a regular feature. The shortage of eggs encouraged housewives to turn to poultry keeping. Even women who lived in terraced houses in towns and cities kept a few hens in their back yards. Yet in spite of the hardship caused by rationing, women would get together to help out on special occasions. Margaret Walsh's wedding cake was made with ingredients contributed by a number of friends and family (see also pp. 97, 98, 109).

The Government aimed a barrage of propaganda at the housewife. They exhorted her to save fuel whether cooking or doing the weekly wash. The Ministry of Agriculture urged her to 'Dig for victory' telling her to 'turn your garden over to vegetables. Get your older children to help'. If she did not have a garden she was told to get an allotment and a character called 'Mrs Sew and Sew' encouraged her to 'make do and mend'. Women's magazines kept up the pressure and gave advice on such things as how to turn a worn sheet, by cutting it down the middle and sewing the two less worn sides together in a central seam. If all that was not enough, advertisements for knitting wool urged her to make knitting her national service. It is little wonder that many housewives longed for the end of the war and a return to normal life.

The importance of being cheerful

During the war 'keeping cheerful' was elevated almost to the status of a national duty by the propaganda machine. 'Keep smiling through', sang Vera Lynn in the popular song 'We'll meet again'. Even the advertisers took up the theme. Beecham's Pills wooed customers with the phrase 'To keep you smiling in times like these' and Bovril used the slogan 'The cup that cheers'. Being cheerful involved putting on a brave face and for a woman this meant make-up. Women were urged to be as attractive as they could as part of the war effort. Women's magazines urged them to keep up appearances for the sake of their men and their country, and they gave many tips on coping when cosmetics were rationed. The radio also dispensed advice on beauty with such items as 'Beauty in battledress' and 'All-weather faces'.

Keeping up appearances was not easy. In the final part of her autobiography, *Lime Street at Two*, Helen Forrester described a problem caused by clothes rationing. When stockings were rationed she and her colleagues stopped wearing

OPPOSITE
This Ministry of Food advertisement from c.1945 was just one of the many placed in magazines to help wives and mothers deal with the problems of food shortages. Note the reference to 'mock cream' in the box.

Dame Vera Lynn, 1917–

The name Vera Lynn is invariably connected with the Second World War. Known as 'the forces' sweetheart', she was the most popular singer during the war and in 1939/40 was voted top singer in the *Daily Express* newspaper. Her importance to the war effort was inestimable, and songs like 'The white cliffs of Dover' and 'We'll meet again' stirred patriotism and lifted morale. During the war she hosted the popular radio show *Sincerely Yours*, which ran until 1947. She also toured Burma in 1944 entertaining the troops.

Although she was only twenty-two when war broke out, she was no stranger to the limelight. Born Vera Margaret Welch on 20 March 1917 in East Ham, London, she first sang in public at the age of seven. When she was 11 she joined a dancing troupe and by 15 she was involved in running a small dancing school. In 1935 she started recording with Joe Loss, then went on to work with Charlie Kunz. From 1937 to 1940 she sang with the Ambrose Orchestra.

Her popularity continued after the war and in 1952 she became the first British artiste to reach the top of the US hit parade with 'Auf Wiederseh'n, Sweetheart', which sold 12 million copies. Over the years Vera appeared in seven Royal Variety Performances and in 1984, the fortieth anniversary of the D-Day landings, her album *20 Family Favourites* was in the British top thirty. In recognition of her service to the country she was made a Dame of the British Empire in 1975. She received the Freedom of the City of London in 1978 and was awarded the Burma Star in 1985.

them and stained their legs with gravy browning instead. This was a common practice and before long enterprising cosmetic manufacturers latched onto the idea and created leg make-up. The management at Helen's workplace, however, insisted that women had to wear stockings at work. The women offered to wear trousers instead but this caused even more outrage. The management only relented after the women threatened to resign en masse.

Good morale was recognised as being of vital importance to the war effort, but it was not easy to achieve. The M-O report on morale, referred to above, painted a gloomy picture of morale in a number of bombed cities including Manchester.

The report was rejected by some, but Margaret Gladwin (later Walsh), who worked in the city, spoke of a terrible atmosphere of fear, especially during air raids, and the sense that normal life was put on hold. Liverpool was one of the few cities where morale remained high. The report concluded that this was due, in part, to the resilience of its women. Liverpool had been one of the worst affected cities during the Depression and its women, as Helen Forrester's autobiography shows, had become used to dealing with deprivation. Many of them were also used to managing alone during the long absences of husbands who went to sea.

It is hardly surprising to learn that women's spirits were sometimes low, especially in the cities. Their lives were disrupted, they spent hours queuing for essential items and they had to face the bombing raids. Even if they were fortunate enough to escape a direct hit, after a raid they were often faced by a house covered in dust and even soot shaken from its chimneys by the blasts. Those with husbands and children away from home were often lonely and worried about their families. It was also difficult to keep cheerful when nights were spent in shelters and bombing raids disrupted sleep. Morale tended to be lower among older women with heavier responsibilities, but younger women also were affected. Margaret Gladwin's job with the Post Office was often depressing as she worked in the department that sent out telegrams to the families of soldiers killed or missing in action. It was worse on the days when a telegram went to a family she knew.

Although places of entertainment shut at the start of the war they were soon reopened and played an important part in raising morale. Young women, especially, took advantage of the more relaxed attitudes to go out and enjoy themselves, though many preferred to stay at home during the blackout. Margaret Gladwin, who was only fifteen when war broke out, enjoyed going to the cinema and dances but she went in the afternoons. My aunt, Doris Reilly (later Close; see also box on p.98) was another young woman who loved to dance, and she and her friends went dancing whenever they could. Her determination to live life to the full, which she never lost, she attributed to a near-miss experience during an air raid.

People also made their own entertainment. The AFS station where Betty Turner worked put on an annual concert party, open to the general public. The entertainment was deliberately kept light. In one typical comedy routine, a man would trundle on with a lawn mower as Betty danced on stage dressed in a grass skirt. Such light-hearted entertainment served to lift the spirits and boost the morale of both the entertainers and their audience.

'Over sexed and over here'

The war affected women's lives in many ways but for some it was the arrival of servicemen from abroad that had the greatest effect. As a result, many found themselves starting a new life in a new country once the war was over. Although servicemen from several nations were stationed in Britain, it was the Americans who made the most impact. They were highly paid, well dressed, and brought a touch of Hollywood glamour. Their greatest attraction, no doubt, was their access to goods that had become luxuries in Britain.

Margaret Walsh recalled that many Americans would give a woman a pair of nylons just for dancing with them. In Margaret's case, and for many others like her, dancing with the Americans was just innocent fun. Some people, however, feared that in the freer atmosphere of the war the presence of the Americans and their gifts would put young women in moral danger. Women's magazines were quick to warn women not to cheapen themselves, reminding them that they would lose a man's respect and risk their chance of marriage if they did not stay virtuous. Some women, however, were immune to the charms of the Americans. Twenty-seven year old Joan Arkwright, quoted in *Wartime Women*, referred to a group of American soldiers as 'a tough looking gang, grown-up dead end kids'.

Some women met foreign servicemen in the unlikely setting of their own homes, as families often invited lonely servicemen home to a meal. Doris Reilly, a member of the WRNS, met her future husband in this way. In 1945 Doris joined the many women who left Britain to start a new life abroad. She said she was lucky as her husband, Andy Close, had been totally honest about the life she could expect in Canada. She knew of women who crossed the Atlantic to find conditions there very different from what they had been led to expect. Some servicemen, apparently, spun elaborate stories about their lives back home, and women, whose only knowledge of life in North America came from Hollywood, believed what they were told. Some men told their prospective brides that they owned a 'gopher farm', and a number of British women, not knowing that a gopher was a burrowing animal, such as a ground squirrel or a pouched rat, were duly impressed.

Demobilisation

Many women viewed the armistace with mixed feelings. They knew that peace would bring a return to normality and end the disruption brought by war, but it also brought the likelihood of a return to a life in which they would be expected to stay at home. While most women looked forward to the end of the war and its hardships, many were reluctant to give up their independence. A large number of women, including many full-time housewives, had had to make their own decisions during the war and had gained in confidence as a result. Most of them knew, however, that once they returned, their husbands and fiancés would expect decision-making to revert to them.

Women who had been forced into work they did not enjoy or to work 12 hour shifts in factories as well as running a home were among those who looked forward to a life at home. Others, especially professional women and those who enjoyed their work, were unhappy about the prospect of a return of the marriage bar. The fact that women had proved themselves as capable as men in almost every field counted for little. In 1942, to reassure the unions, the Government passed a Restoration of Pre-war Practices Act, which ensured that, at the end of the war, women doing 'men's jobs' would have to leave. Bella Keyzer, cited in *Out of the Doll's House*, was one of them. She was not allowed to continue with her job as a welder once the war was over.

Although women had little choice in the immediate aftermath of the war, many resolved to keep their independence. Emmie Turner, who had served in WRNS in the First World War, told her daughter Betty how restless she, and others like her, felt once the war ended. Betty, who had enjoyed the independence that earning her own money brought, resolved not to suffer the same frustration that came from being tied to the home. There were many others like her, but their attempts to live a more fulfilling life would not be easy. The propaganda was in place to persuade women to believe that their greatest possible achievement was to become perfect wives and mothers.

British GI wives protesting in 1945 at the wait to join their husbands in the USA. These women, however, were among the lucky ones who had married their GI boyfriends. Many others were left with illegitimate babies.

From Housewives' Choice to rock and roll

Few tasks are more like the torture of Sisyphus than housework, with its endless repetition.

SIMONE DE BEAUVOIR, FROM THE SECOND SEX

Nostalgia for the late 1940s and the 1950s, which reached its height during Queen Elizabeth II's golden jubilee in 2002, painted the period as an idyllic one. According to the airbrushed view, it was a time of stability, peace and contentment. There was little fear of crime. Houses could be left unlocked and women could relax knowing that their children were safe playing out on the streets. Images of contented families continued the theme. Prettily dressed mothers played with happy children in spotless houses while proud, pipe-smoking fathers looked on indulgently.

This image, while being highly romanticised, is not simply a creation of the nostalgia industry but has been gleaned from material put out by advertisers and the propaganda of the time. The war had severely disrupted society, nowhere more so than in women's roles, and most men were anxious for a return to the status quo. Men, who had been unhappy to see women forced into what they considered 'unnatural' roles during the war, were anxious to see them return to their 'rightful' place as wives and mothers. There was a concerted effort to persuade women that, in spite of all they had done during the war, they should abdicate responsibility and leave it to a man to care for them.

Fashion played its part in restoring the 'natural' order. Unlike the fashions of the 1920s, which gave women a new freedom, the fashionable look after the Second World War emphasised a woman's frailty and femininity. Dior led the way with his glamorous 'New Look' of 1947. With its pinched in waist, and longer, fuller skirts, it was a look that echoed the tiny waists and crinolines of the Victorian period. Women were encouraged to reject the 'masculine' dress of the war years, with its dungarees, trousers and military uniforms, in favour of clothes that were far removed from the world of men.

It was important, if there was to be a return to the status quo, that women should forget about the jobs that they had proved so capable of doing, so the new fashion was about more than external appearances. With its emphasis on femininity, it would be difficult to imagine a woman wearing the 'New Look' being capable of repairing an aeroplane, felling trees or giving orders. It was above all a demure look. Aristocratic models displayed an ice cool sophistication with an untouchable quality which debutantes did their best to emulate. For others the ideal was to appear bandbox fresh, wholesome and feminine.

The accolade 'feminine' was preferred to 'womanly', which had dangerous connotations of worldliness, sensuality and, possibly, of someone with a mind of her own. Men referred to women of all classes as 'ladies' and the more accurate 'women' was considered rude. By implication, feminine women were entertainingly dizzy and fluffy: they paid a great deal of attention to their appearance and left serious matters to men; most importantly they accepted men as their superiors.

Expectations, marriage and motherhood

Throughout the war the Government had been keen to stress the temporary nature of women's work and through its propaganda machine did its best to persuade women that their most important role was to keep the home going. Even during the war much of the material in women's magazines stressed the importance of a woman retaining her femininity, hence the encouragement to wear

OPPOSITE
In the late 1940s and 1950s, the radio was a popular form of entertainment and popular day-time programmes like Housewives' Choice and Woman's Hour kept women from being bored as they went about their chores, often assisted by their daughters. Girls were encouraged from an early age to help around the house.

Footballers' wives, 1950s style

In the 1950s a woman married to a footballer had none of the aspirations of a modern footballer's wife. In 1951, my aunt, Joan Reilly, married Johnny Huggins, who at the time of their marriage played football for the Navy and part-time for Aldershot. When he left the service, he became a full-time footballer. The change made little difference to Joan's life (women did not have lifestyles then) and, although she had become a professional footballer's wife, she had no celebrity status. She was glad to say that no reporters hovered at her door and no photographers showed the slightest interest in what she wore. In the 1950s the press was interested in how well a footballer played, not in his wife or girlfriend.

Far from being superstars, footballers in the 1950s were simply men with a job to do, and as a result their families were anonymous and invisible. Today a footballer's wife can expect to enjoy designer clothes, jewellery and a luxurious house. There were no such luxuries for Joan. These days, a footballer with one of the top clubs could easily buy an average-priced house from a couple of week's pay. In the 1950s, because footballers had a maximum wage, the highest paid footballer in the country would need almost a month's pay to buy a vacuum cleaner. Although 1950s footballers received bonuses, the rate at Aldershot was £2 for a win and £1 for a draw, hardly the stuff of 'champagne lifestyles'. The majority of players were no better off financially than their friends who worked in other trades, and this ordinariness was reflected in the lives of their wives.

A footballer and his wife: Johnny and Joan Huggins with their young son Michael c.1952. Although Aldershot was in one of the lower divisions, because of the maximum wage which operated until the 1960s, footballers in the higher divisions would not have been paid much more than Johnny.

make-up even with a uniform. At no time were women encouraged to think that the work they did during the war would lead to a career. In most quarters, it was still believed that for a woman marriage and motherhood were careers in themselves.

This belief, which to be fair was also held by many women at the time, affected the way that girls were brought up. The nursery rhyme taught girls that they were made of 'sugar and spice and all things nice'. The rest of the rhyme, which told them that boys were made of 'slugs and snails and puppy dog tails' dissuaded most of them from wanting to be like their brothers. In keeping with the rhyme, girls were expected to be gentle and quiet and, like Janet in the reading scheme prevalent in the 1950s, to enjoy helping mother with her domestic chores.

Not all quiet occupations, however, were equally valued. Playing with dolls, doing jigsaws or helping mother were fine, but reading was suspect. A girl who spent too much time reading was considered a 'bookworm,' a name which, though not derogatory in itself, marked her out as being different. A similar fate awaited an adventurous girl. She was labelled a 'tomboy' and tutted over in despair if she returned from play with scraped knees and torn clothes. A boy who came home looking equally dishevelled would be sighed over in a different way. Unless he was completely out of hand, he was regarded with pride as a 'proper boy'.

Mothers who were unfortunate enough to have a daughter who was both a tomboy and a bookworm were often looked on with pity. Not only were such daughters less helpful in the house, they caused concern because they risked ending up unmarried and 'on the shelf'. A tomboy failed to display the femininity and submissiveness thought necessary to attract a husband, while bookworms, like the 'bluestockings' of an earlier century, were thought to frighten off potential husbands by being too clever. A cartoon published in *Woman* magazine in 1952 reinforced these attitudes. It shows a prettily dressed girl accompanied by two attentive men. As she walks past, a girl in jeans turns to a frumpy girl who is carrying a book and remarks, 'I thought you said she wasn't intelligent'.

For the majority of parents of girls growing up during the 1940s and 1950s, the idea of a woman having a career for life, as opposed to a job for a few years before she married, was difficult to grasp. Even those who encouraged their daughters to pursue their education to a high level still expected them to settle down to marriage. In her memoir, *A House Unlocked*, Penelope Lively recalls that her father, who had seen her go up to Oxford, was so concerned that she was still unmarried at the age of twenty-three that he felt it necessary to discuss the matter with her. Her father was not alone in showing concern about his daughter's marriage prospects. In a letter to Evelyn Home, *Woman* magazine's agony aunt, a mother worried that her twenty-six year old daughter was in danger of ruining her life because she had turned down two offers of marriage, preferring instead to concentrate on her career.

It was the belief that a girl would eventually marry and be supported by her husband that caused many parents to neglect a daughter's education. As there was no shortage of work in shops, offices and factories for a girl without qualifications in this period, many parents were happy for their daughters to leave school at fifteen, a year before Ordinary level General Certificate of Education (GCE) examinations were taken. My parents, who believed in the value of education for its own sake, were often asked why they kept me on at school. Well meaning friends and relatives told them that it was a waste of my time and their money as I would 'only be getting married'. They believed that a girl would be better off earning her keep and saving for her trousseau than gaining 'unnecessary' qualifications.

Education

In spite of the widely held belief that the average girl needed little education beyond the basics, the Education Act of 1944 improved opportunities for many girls by making secondary, as well as elementary, schooling compulsory for all children up to the age of fifteen. This meant that for the first time all girls would receive a secondary education.

In theory, this should have made a huge difference to working class girls' opportunities, but because of the way schools were organised the effect was minimised. The Act created three types of secondary school: grammar, technical and secondary modern. Grammar schools, which took approximately 25 per cent of children, were set up to provide an academic education which would lead to a university place for the brightest of its pupils. Technical schools were designed for those with a practical ability and were better at catering for boys who wished to go into engineering and similar occupations. Secondary moderns were for the rest.

In theory, because selection was on the basis of ability and not the ability to pay, working class girls had an equal chance of receiving an academic education. Yet much depended on their primary schools, as not all of them made an effort to prepare their pupils for the 11 Plus, the examination which decided the type of secondary school they could go to. It is interesting that in 1949 *The Lady* wrote an opinion piece against selection at 11. It mentioned Churchill and Einstein as people who would have been condemned to a third-rate education under the new system, but made no mention of the effect on girls.

The curriculum in a girls' grammar school was similar, if not identical, to that for boys. Girls learned Latin and modern languages as well as the full range of sciences; domestic science and needlework were rarely included. Girls were

encouraged to be competitive and academic and were expected to take Ordinary ('O') and Advanced ('A') level GCEs. Although many girls gained the qualifications necessary to enter university only a few bothered to apply. Some ended their education after taking 'A' levels because of parental pressure. Others, at a time when women married young, left because they wanted a few years of independence earning their own money before marrying and settling down to raise a family.

Girls in technical schools had a more vocational training but their curriculum was very different from that of the boys. Technical schools were less relevant to girls as they were not encouraged to do engineering or mechanics. For them, technical training involved shorthand and typing or hairdressing skills. Secondary modern schools were the worst. They were often in old buildings with few facilities. The majority of schools were single sex schools, but many in the secondary modern sector were mixed. Although there were dedicated teachers, a few had low expectations of their pupils and spoke to them with little disguised contempt. Small wonder that many girls were reduced to tears when they heard that they had failed the II Plus.

There were, however, a few excellent secondary schools that, because of an enlightened headteacher and dedicated staff, refused to write off their pupils. At

A fourth form class in Oak Park County Secondary Girls' School in 1957. The teacher, Mrs Blockley, persuaded most of the girls in her form to stay for an extra year to take public examinations. In the 1950s it was very unusual for secondary school girls to be encouraged in this way. The author is in the back row, third from left.

Cambridge awards degrees to women

In 1948, twenty-eight years after Oxford first awarded degrees to its women students, Cambridge University finally followed suit. On 15 November 1948, *The Times* reported on the ceremony in which women, including many who had left Cambridge years before, received their degrees. The Queen was the first woman to receive a degree from Cambridge; she was awarded an honorary degree of Doctor of Law. It is ironic that the first woman to be awarded a degree by the university had never studied there.

Girton students outside the Stanley Library after the award of their degrees from Cambridge in 1948.

Oak Park County Secondary Girls' School in Havant, for example (see photograph on p. 105), the staff encouraged girls to make the most of their abilities. The more academically inclined girls were set homework and encouraged to stay on an extra year to take 'O' levels, which was unusual in secondary moderns. As Biology was the only science taught in the school, arrangements were made for any girls showing an aptitude for the sciences to take Physics and Chemistry 'O' level at the adjacent boys' school. They also provided shorthand and typing lessons for girls interested in taking up office work. In some ways schools like this were the forerunner of the comprehensive schools.

In most secondary moderns the curriculum was weighted in favour of 'girls' subjects: domestic science and needlework took up a fifth of the timetable. Girls were taught hygiene, basic cooking skills and how to clean a house. They were also taught how to wash and iron different materials. Some schools set up a section of the domestic science room as a room where the girls could practise dusting, polishing and setting a table. Others provided a furnished house nearby for girls to practise their housecraft skills. For many of the girls domestic science and needlework were the most relevant lessons.

The 'happy housewife'

Having their own home for most girls meant becoming a housewife, but while they dreamed of dresses of white satin, few appreciated what being a housewife entailed. Although secondary schools worked hard to prepare girls for a life in the home, half a day a week in a domestic science lesson could not fully prepare a girl for the realities of life as a housewife and mother. For grammar school girls there was little or no preparation.

As was the case during the war, there was no shortage of advice for housewives in the women's magazines, which were filled with tips, recipes and advertisements offering products to help achieve the perfect home. The advertisements often came with hidden warnings of what could happen to their families if they failed to do their jobs properly. Children might be bullied and husbands tempted to stray unless a housewife was vigilant. In one advertisement, Surf washing powder came to the rescue of a bullied child by turning a greying white blouse into a sparkling white one. In another, a husband who stayed late at the office was happy to come home early once his wife had made it a more welcoming place by using Zal disinfectant.

The image of the 'happy housewife', who whisked through her chores with a smile and a feather duster, was intended to persuade women that life spent at home was rewarding. However, Betty Storey found images of women waving feather dusters, while wearing glamorous clothes topped by a frilly apron, irritating and an insult to her intelligence. She would not own a feather duster on principle and, refusing to be tied to the house, found a job as a school secretary. Although her stance was unusual in the 1950s, her husband approved, saying that she was a much nicer person when she had a job.

Although many women must have felt as Betty did, the advertisements continued to be a regular feature in the magazines of the period. One for a floor polish, which appeared in the mid 1950s, showed a woman, wearing a tiny apron over an outfit that could have come from Dior, gazing in rapture at the highly polished floor of her kitchen. Another depicted a smiling woman seated on a swing. Over her head was the slogan, 'In the spring housewives sing, Vim makes spring-cleaning go with a swing'.

The reality, of course, was very different and, while she was cleaning the house, a housewife was more likely to be dressed like Andy Capp's wife Flo in a wrap-around apron and turban, than like a debutante off to a garden party. Before vacuum cleaners, housework was a dusty occupation and women wore turbans or headscarves to keep their hair dust-free while sweeping and dusting. The advertisements for vacuum cleaners, which showed a woman overcome with joy, were the closest to reality. In the 1950s owning one was at the top of most women's wish list: they revolutionised housework, making it cleaner, easier and quicker.

Although in the mid 1950s Mrs Thatcher claimed that, properly organised, housework was not arduous, it is difficult to see how anyone would have much free time unless they had paid help and labour saving devices. Bed making, for example, took more effort in the days before duvets and fitted sheets, and blankets created more dust. Without a washing machine or nearby launderette, the weekly wash took at least half a day, and ironing, before easy care fabrics, was also more of a chore. Housework generally took more time and Sally Everest, who taught Domestic Science in the 1950s (see also p. 125), calculated that it would be difficult, without a vacuum cleaner and spray polishes, to clean a room thoroughly in under an hour.

According to Sally, the routines set out in the *Housewives' Book*, published in the 1930s, were still in use in the 1950s. An efficient housewife would start her day at 7 a.m and finish at 8.30 p.m. In the winter months, even in some houses with central heating, many started their day by cleaning out a fire-grate and lighting a fire. After she had prepared breakfast, a housewife would have to make the beds, clean the house and do the shopping. As she would be unlikely to have a refrigerator, she shopped for food several times a week, if not every day. As many children and husbands came home for their midday meal, she could also produce three meals a day.

In addition, she had to find time to do her weekly chores, which included

washing ... ɔm in the house
had to ... ng the floor and
furnitur ... kes, scones and
pastries ... fruit and made
pickles, ... be done while
looking

Altl ... nd did nothing.
There w ... to be taken up.
Until cl ... s salvaged worn
clothes ... ɛgs of a pair of
trousers ... a girl's pleated
skirt. Ev ... ' continued for
some tin ... suit made from
a woollel

Of ... were far from
efficient housewives, but a woman who did not at least keep her home and children
clean was likely to be gossiped about. For those who enjoyed domesticity, the role
of housewife was an enjoyable career and many took a great pride in doing it well.
For women who had spent the years before they married in dull or 'dead end' jobs,
becoming a housewife was often a change for the better.

Work outside the home

While many women enjoyed running their homes, others who were less
domesticated felt differently. A file in the National Archives (LAB 8/2379) dealing
with the social implications of married women's work gives some of the reasons
why women chose to work outside the home. It refers to 'mental and emotional
satisfaction ... some financial independence ... companionship and new interests
outside the home'. Although the report does not spell it out, another reason is
implicit: quite simply, many women disliked housework, finding it tedious and
unrewarding.

Married women who wanted to work found the economic climate in their
favour. Instead of the economic slump of the 1920s and 1930s, which had led to the
marriage bar and forced women back into the home, in the late 1940s and 1950s
there was a shortage of labour, which made the employment of women essential. In
the file mentioned above, there is a telling comment that although industry
complained of the disadvantages in employing married women it 'could not do
without them'. In many places the marriage bar melted away and it became
acceptable for a married woman to work until her first pregnancy.

Jill Craigie (1914-1999)

Jill Craigie, who was born in Derbyshire on 7 March 1914, led a remarkable life for a woman born at that time. Although she married three times, and had a child, she still managed to have a career as an actress, film director and writer. As a director, Jill made a number of influential films. In *The Way We Live* (1945), she dealt with the reconstruction of Plymouth after the war and included ordinary people's lives. In 1948 she formed her own production company, Outlook Productions, and produced her only fictional film, *Blue Scar* (1949), which told of the lives and hardships of Welsh miners in the newly nationalised mining industry. The film was highly controversial but, in spite of attempts to ban its release, proved popular. Its success, together with that of *The Way We Live*, proved that there was an audience for films dealing with social issues.

She returned to the documentary format in 1950 for what is arguably her most influential work. In *To Be a Woman* she put the case for equal pay. Her film had more impact than many of the speeches and pamphlets on the subject, and it is interesting that equal pay for civil servants and teachers followed soon after. She did not make another film until almost fifty years later when, in collaboration with her husband, Michael Foot, and financed by their own money, she made *Two Hours from London* which dealt with the Bosnian war.

Although Jill gave up film making soon after her marriage to Michael Foot and was a constant support to her husband, she was far from a traditional wife. She continued to write and was an active campaigner for the left. With Michael Foot, she was one of the founders of the Campaign for Nuclear Disarmament in 1958, and was often to be seen with him at the front of Aldermaston marches. She was deeply interested in the suffrage movement and compiled an impressive collection of suffrage material. She became an authority on the suffragettes and wrote the introduction to the Virago edition of Emmeline Pankhurst's *My Own Story*, which she had encouraged them to republish.

With Stanley Spencer, 1943.

The Government was in a difficult position. It would have preferred women to stay at home (this is proved by the continuation of its marriage bar until late in 1946), but labour shortages meant that it needed to encourage married women to go out to work. Ironically, its policies were partly responsible for the shortages. While admirable in concept, the new welfare state created many jobs in 'female' areas of work and the raising of the school leaving age both exacerbated the labour shortage and increased the demand for teachers. Although women were forced to leave their jobs in the 'male' industries at the end of the war most of them were able to find other work.

The shortages of labour, especially in textiles, forced the Government to campaign for women to return to work. On 30 January 1948, *The Times* reported on a press conference given by Sir Stafford Cripps, the Chancellor of the Exchequer, in which he discussed women and the national effort. According to the report, women had been recruited for 19,000 part-time and 7,500 full-time jobs but the textile industries needed another 30,000 workers. It also reported that, in order to attract married women, factories in Lancashire were opening laundries on their premises. Although women had traditionally worked after marriage in the textile industry, it is interesting that the Chancellor addressed his appeal to men as well as women. Clearly, it was not politic to make a direct appeal to married women without reference to their husbands.

Shortages in industry were not only on the factory floor. A file in the National Archives (LAB 12/585) shows that there was also a shortage of women factory inspectors. To help them to recruit more women, the Government turned to the heads of women's colleges. Correspondence in the file over the period 1949–50 shows that men believed the shortage was caused by women avoiding jobs that 'call for an understanding or appreciation of mechanical and other technical problems'. The heads of the women's colleges pointed out that the higher starting age of 23 and the lack of equality in pay and conditions of service were probably the real reasons why women did not apply.

The Government was concerned enough about the shortage of women recruits to reduce the starting age to 21, but did nothing in the short term to deal with the issue of equal pay. Neither did they do anything to allay fears about conditions of service. These made women cautious about applying for jobs in industry. In her memoir Penelope Lively recalls that women entering commerce or industry were expected to have shorthand and typing qualifications in addition to their degree. As no such requirement was made of male graduates seeking similar jobs, women were naturally 'suspicious about the roles we would be playing if we fell for this discrimination'.

The labour shortage caused problems for many government departments, and indirectly this helped girls in secondary schools. While many of them were still destined for the shop or factory floor, more were being recruited into offices and there was discussion of training some of them to be teachers. With these opportunities opening up it is little wonder that few girls were interested in low paid or domestic work of any kind. In order to fill vacancies in the lowest paid jobs, the Government was forced to turn elsewhere and, with the same lack of enthusiasm it showed during the war, it began to accept women from the Caribbean.

A file in the National Archives (LAB 8/6) deals with the employment of women from Jamaica and Barbados as hospital domestics during the early 1950s. In spite of an initial group of women from Barbados proving satisfactory, with some being promoted to nursing trainees, the authorities seemed reluctant to take more than a token 20 to 25 women from Jamaica. Their excuse was that the supply of domestic staff had improved.

The majority of women continued to receive low wages, with the lowest pay going to female immigrants and part-timers, but the years of campaigning for equal pay finally paid off for some women in the public sector. In the mid 1950s

Equal pay was a burning issue for many women and, during the late 1940s and 1950s, they organised a number of protests against the Government's refusal to grant it to public servants. In this protest, they marched from Westminster to Trafalgar Square.

women teachers, civil servants and local government officers won equal pay, at least in the lower grades. Women, however, who were employed in 'all women' jobs such as nursing and typing, together with women in industry and those employed by private employers, were not entitled to equal pay. Equal pay, though welcomed, did not bring an immediate end to discrimination, as it was still difficult for women to win promotion.

Working mothers

Although the economic situation prevented the Government from pushing all married women back into the home, it was determined to make it as difficult as possible for mothers, especially those with young children, to go out to work. After the war, councils were forced to close their nurseries as the Government first cut and then abolished their funding. As a result, mothers who were unable to make other arrangements were forced to give up their jobs. A paper in a National Archives file (LAB 8/2379) states that, 'It is generally accepted that the employment of mothers with young children is at best a necessary evil and to be discouraged'. The paper added that the Ministry of Labour, the TUC, employers, teachers and social workers, were all of this opinion.

The Government's stance on working mothers was in part due to its concern about the birth rate, which had fallen during the war: it wanted young married women to stay at home and raise a family. In 1947, partly to encourage women to have children, it introduced family allowances, though at a much lower rate than Eleanor Rathbone (see p. 74) had proposed in 1917. Initially the allowance was going to be paid to fathers but the Government backed down in face of fierce opposition, especially from women MPs. As the payment was partly an attempt to boost the birth rate, no payment was made for the first child. It was a very different allowance from that envisaged by Eleanor Rathbone who had seen it as a way of making mothers more independent.

Public opinion towards working mothers was hostile. A paper in the National Archives file mentioned above gives the reasons for this hostility. It states that they were blamed for 'neglect of husbands and children, lack of interest in maintaining high standards in the home, juvenile delinquency and the bad effect on the health of mothers and children'. The same paper, however, revealed that a study in Glasgow 'does indeed prove the opposite on certain points – for example, the employment of mothers is not associated with increased delinquency and "morale" is generally better in these families'.

Some of the hostility stemmed from the work of child psychiatrists, like John Bowlby, who argued that it was psychologically damaging for a young child to be separated from its mother for any length of time. These views were influential on mothers in the 1950s who were often plagued with guilt if they left their children to go to work. Not all mothers agreed with these ideas, however, and several continued to work. Margaret Thatcher, who is quoted by Martin Pugh *in Women and the Women's Movement in Britain*, made her views clear. She wrote of children, 'When looking after them without a break, it is sometimes difficult not to get a little impatient... Whereas, having been out, every moment spent with them is a pleasure to anticipate'.

The rock and roll years

There were many reasons why women wanted to go out to work, and the end of rationing and the growing number of goods in the shops provided another. The document in the National Archives file LAB 8/2379 claims that many married women worked for 'extras' and 'to keep up with the Joneses'. By the second half of the 1950s, the rise in consumerism was changing attitudes towards what were considered essentials. People were beginning to want more than the basic requirements for survival such as adequate housing and sufficient food and clothing; many were beginning to count household gadgets and televisions among the necessities of life.

The new household gadgets not only saved the housewife time so that she could at least take on a part-time job, they often provided the stimulus to find work so that she could afford them. Although some husbands preferred a stay-at-home wife, many were beginning to appreciate the 'extras' that a wife's wages could buy. The increase in the ownership of household gadgets and television sets would have been much slower without the contribution of a woman's wage and, for the better off family, a wife's income made luxuries like foreign holidays possible.

For young women, the rise in consumerism coincided with the arrival of rock and roll and the emergence of the 'teenager'. Fashions changed and shirtwaister dresses worn with yards of flouncy, scratchy, net petticoats gave way to knee-length pencil skirts. The more daring girls adopted what had been thought of as boys' clothing and wore jeans and 'sloppy joes', the name for a long shapeless jumper. The older generation reacted against this fashion, insisting that they could no longer tell the difference between boys and girls. Some fathers banned their daughters from wearing jeans or trews, as women's trousers were sometimes called, and parents feared the bad influence of rock music with its sexual overtones. In the mid 1950s a lucky few were able to shop in Mary Quant's new boutique in Chelsea (see also p. 132). Even then her designs were young and sexy but the majority of women would not come under her influence until the 1960s.

While women still married young, many were determined to enjoy the years before they settled down. They were still taught that 'nice girls didn't' and that men did not marry 'shop-soiled' goods, but attitudes were slowly changing, at least among some young women if not yet in society generally. Penelope Lively realised that a change occurred in attitudes during the mid 1950s, for, while her father was concerned that she was still single at twenty-three, she was not. From Fay Weldon's memoir, *Auto da Fay*, it is clear that that, in the 1950s, some girls

A young couple jiving in 1956. Note the girl's trousers or 'trews'. Many fathers banned their daughters from dressing in trousers, but had they seen the amount of leg revealed (and the occasional flash of underwear) when girls jived wearing flared skirts, they might well have removed their ban.

Rosalind Franklin (1920–1958)

Rosalind Franklin was a brilliant scientist whose work in the 1950s played an important part in the discovery of the structure of DNA. If her father had had his way, however, this discovery could have been delayed for some time, as he wanted her to live a very different life. Born in London in July 1920, Rosalind was a highly intelligent girl who shone in the sciences during her time at St Paul's Girl's School. Although she wanted to be a scientist from an early age, her father initially refused to

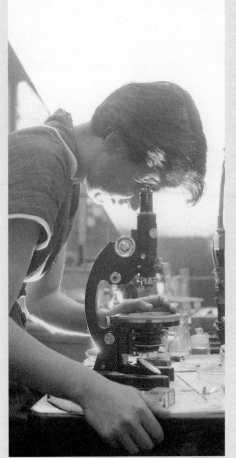

allow her to continue her education. He believed that women should marry, have a family and occupy themselves with charitable and good works. She insisted on continuing her education and in 1938 she went to Newnham College, Cambridge, where she graduated in 1941.

She subsequently spent many years working as a research scientist, studying carbon. Her work in this field eventually led to the development of carbon fibre technology. In 1947, she went to work in Paris where she developed an expertise in x-ray photography. She returned to King's College, London, in 1951 where she applied her skill to research on the structure of DNA. She was close to completing her research when Francis Crick and James Watson, two Cambridge scientists, published their findings on the structure on DNA. Unknown to Rosalind, they had been able to complete their research first because they had had access to her material, including a crucial x-ray photograph.

In 1962, Watson and Crick were awarded the Nobel Prize for Physiology and Medicine for their discovery. The prize was shared with Maurice Wilkins who had worked with Rosalind on DNA at King's, but no mention was made of her work even though its importance was known by all three of the prize-winners. Indeed, it was information from her research, some of which was passed on by Wilkins, which had enabled Crick and Watson to complete their work ahead of her. Rosalind never knew that her contribution had been ignored as she died of ovarian cancer in 1958.

Her part in the discovery might have remained hidden but for the publication in 1968 of James Watson's book, *Double Helix*. In it he made light of her contribution and made patronising and derogatory comments about her appearance. His book provoked a response from her friends and her part in the discovery was revealed in Anne Sayre's *Rosalind Franklin and DNA* in 1975. In recent years Rosalind has been held up as a role model for women in science and the DTI has funded the Rosalind Franklin Medal, an annual prize to be awarded, in conjunction with the Royal Society, to a researcher, male or female, leading the field in scientific research. Part of the award is to be used for the promotion of women in SET (science, engineering and technology). It was fitting that in 2003, fifty years after the discovery of the structure of DNA, a woman, Professor Susan Gibson, won the first Franklin medal.

living away from home were prepared to sleep with their boyfriends, but she also writes of the fear of pregnancy that haunted them each month. She became pregnant but rather than marry the father, risk an abortion, or have the baby adopted, she decided to keep it. This was almost unheard of behaviour in the 1950s and she was persuaded to change her name by deed poll to Mrs Davies in order to avoid the child being known as a 'bastard', and to maintain some aura of respectability.

For the majority of women, however, heavy petting was as far as they would go. Fear of pregnancy and the shame attached to illegitimacy stopped most of them from 'going all the way'. Very few women went to university and most lived at home until they married so had very little freedom. The lack of reliable contraception was another factor as family planning clinics were strictly for married women. It was not till some time after the arrival of the pill in the next decade that single women would be able to enjoy sex without fear.

Dolly birds and double standards

The freedom women were supposed to have in the Sixties largely boiled down to easy contraception and abortion: things to make life easier for men, in fact.

JULIE BURCHILL

For the people who did not live through them, and for a few who did, the image of the 'swinging sixties' has taken on a mythic quality. The 1960s 'dolly bird' has gone down in history as a fun-seeking, free-loving 'swinger'. Like her 'flapper' sisters in the 1920s, she shocked the older generation with the shortness of her skirts and her wild behaviour. The 'dolly bird' danced all night in discotheques filled with the heavy scent of illegal substances and relaxed between dances on mattresses strategically placed in dark corners. She inhabited an egalitarian milieu and was equally at ease with dukes or dustmen. Home was often a bed-sit or flat share, preferably in 'Swinging London', and well away from parental control. She worked in offices where she was chosen for the length of her skirts rather than the speed of her shorthand. Her promiscuity broke up marriages and, in the case of Christine Keeler and Mandy Rice-Davies, brought down a government.

The fashions of the time certainly gave the impression that women were sexually available. During the 1960s, skirts had shrunk so much that some joked they were little more than a wide belt, while young men fondly referred to them as 'pussy warmers' or 'pussy pelmets'. They were soon followed by hot pants, which were short, clingy and left little to the imagination. The bikini, which had been quite shocking when it first appeared in 1946, became old-fashioned, and on the beach the brave and the beautiful went topless.

'Pussy Galore' and other images of women

Much of the myth was created by the images of the time. Fashion photography broke away from the elegance of the 1950s and Mary Quant (see profile, p. 132) insisted that her models be photographed in provocative poses. In an interview for the *Guardian* in 1967, she said that the intention of fashion photography was to shock and went on to claim that 'pornography is great if it's good'. Her definition of good pornography was 'erotic but pleasing'. Models in her clothes looked confident and self-assured, and their direct gaze challenged the onlooker. Although they looked sexually available it was very much on their terms.

Pussy Galore (played by Honor Blackman) points a gun at James Bond in the film *Goldfinger*, 1964.

Images in the 1960s were anything but demure. One of the most compelling of the decade is the photograph of Christine Keeler, clearly naked yet covered by the chair she sits astride. In an earlier decade a prostitute would have been vilified as a 'fallen woman'; in the 1960s she acquired celebrity status. Marianne Faithfull's film, *Girl on a Motorcycle*, celebrated a woman's freedom to do as she pleased. In the film *Darling*, Julie Christie played a woman who was prepared to use sex to get what she wanted – and she wanted everything.

Although many of the images of the 1960s showed women to be confident and in control, there were contradictions within that image. The Bond girl, Pussy Galore, who flew an aeroplane and led a team of women pilots, though feisty and confident was at the same time shown to be vulnerable and susceptible to Bond's dubious charm. The television series *The Avengers* carried the concept of confident and independent women further. Although they were first and foremost attractive women, Honor Blackman, Diana Rigg and Linda Thorsen all played characters who were capable of looking after themselves in most situations. Though the

OPPOSITE
Yorkshire Miners' Coal Queen at National Union of Mineworkers gala at Doncaster in 1968. Although all are arguably 'dolly birds', the girl on the left's shift dress and shorter skirt is most typical of 1960s fashion.

situations were unrealistic, the women were shown holding their own against men, even when fighting, and occasionally they were allowed to rescue the male leads.

Widening horizons

As the decade progressed, some women, inspired by the confidence and freedom epitomised by icons like Marianne Faithfull (see photograph, p. 131), began to believe that they too could do anything and go anywhere. Their confidence was boosted by the ease of finding work, especially for those with office or secretarial skills. In London at least a phone call to an agency could bring work as a temp within days. English secretaries and receptionists were also highly prized in the USA: an agency even allowed girls to combine work with travel, offering to find temporary work for them in whichever state they were visiting.

An office worker of the 1960s.

It was not only those with secretarial skills who found work abroad. In July 1963, *Woman's Own* ran a feature on women working abroad as part of a series on careers. It featured a nurse, a receptionist and two teachers. All were in traditional jobs yet the fact that they had travelled abroad to work was novel. Their new found confidence also meant that women were travelling more widely either alone (few had any fears on this score) or with friends. Diana Shelley, a secretary from London, went to Israel, where she worked on a kibbutz and hitchhiked around the country by herself. Carol Allen (later McCormick Smith; see also p. 130), who worked in sales and in an employment agency, said that during the 1960s she felt fired by a sense of freedom. She worked for a time as an au pair in Italy and said that travel, which had once been seen as exotic, was becoming commonplace.

The expansion of the universities in the 1960s meant that more young, though mostly middle class, women went on to higher education with the resultant freedom and greater opportunities which that brought. Even though the majority of women were still employed in teaching, nursing or secretarial work these were no longer thought of stopgaps until marriage but were described as careers. In July 1963, *Woman's Own* also reported on a man who looked after his four children in term time, while his wife took a degree at Liverpool University.

Although this reflects a shift in attitudes, the fact that it was reported shows that it was unusual enough to be considered newsworthy.

The 1960s also saw women reaping the benefits of the struggle of earlier generations to enter the professions, and several of them were reaching the heights in their chosen careers. In 1964, Dorothy Crowfoot Hodgkin won the Nobel Prize for Chemistry for her research on the vitamin B_{12}. Her achievement was even more remarkable as she had continued to work in the 1930s and 1940s despite being a wife and mother. The following year, forty-three years after Dr Ivy Williams became the first woman to be called to the English Bar, Dame Elizabeth Lane became the first woman High Court judge.

Other women were branching out into what were traditionally male fields. In 1964 *Woman* ran a story on Gwen Moffat who had become the first official female mountain guide; her advice, 'never make a man look silly', speaks volumes. Dame Patricia Hornsby-Smith MP became the first woman chairman of a unit trust at a time when women were not allowed on the floor of the stock exchange. Mary Quant, who turned her small boutique into a fashion empire, proved that women could be entrepreneurs. She was not alone in her success. By the mid 1960s, Margery Hurst's Brook Street Bureau, which she had started in a tiny room in Mayfair, was the largest secretarial agency in the world.

Even some of those who stayed at home were showing entrepreneurial skills. In August 1966, *The Times* published an article about a group of seven mothers who, early in the decade, had decided to launch a project together. They formed Septima Ltd and published *What's On for Children and Young People* which covered the Home Counties. The publication was successful and there were demands for it to expand to cover the whole country. The group, feeling that their family commitments made this impossible, sold the publication for 'four figures'. They continued with other projects and in 1966 produced a book of children's activities, *Something to Do*, which was published by Penguin. Although the women had not wanted to go out to work, they claimed that their group enterprises had saved them from 'cabbagehood'. They were reported as saying that, 'our husbands find us better people', a sentiment that echoed Betty Storey's words (see p. 107) in the 1950s.

Birth control and abortion

Arguably the single most influential event on women's lives in the twentieth century was the advent of the contraceptive pill, first available in 1961. Its greatest benefit was its near 100% reliability and the fact that it put women in control of their fertility. It enabled them to plan their families, which in turn meant that they

Metropolitan policewomen in their new uniforms, 1967. An increasing number of women joined the police force during the 1960s though they were largely confined to dealing with families and juveniles – areas considered suitable for female officers.

could plan their careers. As a result, it became easier to persuade employers to take them seriously. In general, the pill's reliability made women more relaxed about sex, enabling them to associate it with recreation instead of procreation. Possibly for this reason, many people attribute the rise of the permissive society to the development of the pill.

The effect of the pill on single women in the 1960s, however, has been exaggerated. For most of the decade it was difficult for them to obtain this or other reliable contraceptives. Family planning clinics dealt only with married women or those about to be married, and they questioned single women in depth, wanting details of their fiancés. They only relaxed this attitude at the very end of the period. Even in the second half of the 1960s, few single women took the pill. *Out of the Doll's House* quotes an anonymous 'swinger' as saying that the pill was more talked about than taken. Carol Allen, who was very much part of the

'Swinging London' scene, said that in 1967, although she was vaguely aware of the pill, neither she nor any of her friends took it. Some single women, however, were taking it. In March 1967, *The Times* reported that a firm, Step One Ltd, was charging single women a fee of £2 for the name of a doctor who would supply them with the pill and it estimated that one in ten doctors would prescribe the pill to single girls.

In spite of the pill, the 1960s saw a rise in the number of illegitimate births. This rise reflected not only an increase in pre-marital sex but also a change in attitudes. Many women who in earlier generations would have been persuaded to marry the father of their child, rejected a shotgun marriage and put their baby up for adoption. In other cases, illegitimate children were born to couples who were living as man and wife even though they were not married. In these cases the couples kept their children and few knew that they were illegitimate. One of the reasons for the change in the divorce law in 1969 was to enable such couples to marry and legitimise their children.

Many women who found themselves pregnant during the 1960s resorted to abortion, and, although estimates vary, it is thought that around 100,000 illegal abortions were performed in Britain each year. Although a legal medical termination was available in very limited circumstances, for the rest it was illegal: both the mother and the person who assisted her to terminate a pregnancy could be jailed. In spite of this, abortions by qualified doctors were available, though they were usually very expensive.

A pregnant woman who was poor, and desperate to avoid having a child, often felt that she had no choice but to have an abortion. Such a decision had to be an act of desperation as the chances of death or permanent injury from a back street abortion were high. Many of the back-street abortionists had no medical qualifications whatsoever, though several claimed to be doctors. Details of a case against one such bogus doctor can be seen in a file in the National Archives (MEPO 2/10945). The file deals with the police enquiry into the practices of a 'Doctor' Stanley Robert Martin who was charged and later found guilty of the manslaughter by 'septic abortion' of Nurse Edna May Roberts.

The horrors of a back street abortion are illustrated by the description of 'Doctor' Martin's surgery. The report describes the filthy conditions of his premises and instruments, and gives graphic details of his unhygienic methods. It was not surprising to read that several of the women who went to him ended up in hospital. It is clear from the file that the police felt sure Edna Roberts was not the only woman to have died as result of his practices. They had no proof, however, as people were very reluctant to admit to any knowledge of abortion to the police. Many of the women whose names were found at his premises denied going to him for an abortion; a few went so far as to say that he was a good doctor.

Information from a list of more than a hundred of his clients suggests that contraception was still not widely practised throughout society. Many of the women on the list, more than half of whom were married, already had several children. Even some of the single women had already had a child. It was in order to reduce the reliance of such women on back street abortionists that the 1967 Abortion Law was passed. Although this law did not allow abortion on demand, it did allow doctors to consider social grounds when deciding whether or not to terminate a pregnancy. The vagueness of the wording in the Act, however, caused a great deal of disquiet. Objectors feared that the lack of clarity as to what constituted social grounds would open the door to abortion on demand.

Wives and mothers

Unlike the 1950s, when the predominant image of women was as housewives, images of women in the 1960s tended to centre on the young and single woman. Yet throughout the decade most women married in their early twenties and many married even earlier. When Maureen Pond (later Geary-Andrews; see front jacket, middle photograph) was twenty she joined the WAAF after much hinting from aunts who had been in the services during the war. Years later she realised that, because she worked in an all-female office and had no steady boyfriend, her family had been worried about her chances of getting married. They felt that she would be in a better position to meet 'a nice young man' and settle down if she joined the services. In the 1960s, especially among the older generation, many women still believed that a woman's function was to marry and have children.

In the 1960s, although it was acceptable for women to stay in their jobs after they married, the majority of employers still expected a woman to resign once she became pregnant. The most usual pattern was for a woman to stay at home as a full-time housewife and mother until her youngest child had at least reached school age. Some would then work part-time so that they could take their children to and from school. Once her children were in their teens, a mother might take a full-time job but many waited until their children had left school – if they returned to work at all.

Life was difficult for mothers who continued to work full time while their children were young, as there was very little provision for child-care. This was due in part to deliberate government policy. A file in the National Archives (LAB 10/1775) contains a report of an international meeting which looked at the topic of women workers in a changing world. The report is a long and complex document but it showed that the UK voted against many measures designed to make it easier for mothers of young children to go out to work, including the provision of child-care.

Mothers who applied for full-time work were often quizzed about their child-care arrangements at interview. Even if their children attended a nursery, they were often asked what they would do when their children were sick. In some jobs, especially in teaching where there was a shortage of qualified staff, mothers were encouraged to work. Teaching was considered an ideal job for a mother because of the hours and holidays. It was more problematic for women with pre-school age children, and Sally Everest had to rely on au pairs until her children were old enough to go to school. In some cases it was a woman's friends and family who were hostile to a working mother. Sally was told that she was a bad mother for continuing to work after she had children, even though she was her family's main breadwinner. As well as needing to work, Sally was one of a growing number of women who were reluctant to give up the career that they had worked long and hard for.

The 1960s were the first decade in which all young women received full-time secondary education, at least up to the age of fifteen. Many had been educated at grammar or independent schools and some had taken 'A' levels. There was also a rise in the number of women graduates during the decade. The 1960s housewives were also the first who could take ownership of household gadgets for granted. By the end of the decade almost every home had a vacuum cleaner and many also had a washing machine. As housework became less time-consuming, some stay-at-home wives found that they were bored.

During the decade there was a rise in the number of female graduates. Glenna Oag, shown here marrying George Knight in 1963, had recently graduated in Botany from the University of Edinburgh, although she chose to give up her job as a lab technician when the first of her four children was born in 1966.

Many women, however, had husbands who were not keen on them returning to work. When Myra Noble, who had worked as an industrial chemist before her marriage, took a part-time job, her husband sent her a bouquet with the message 'congratulations on your retirement'. After a while, finding it difficult to cope with a family and a sea-faring husband who expected her to be at home when he returned on leave, she gave up her job. Myra kept boredom at bay by maintaining a circle of women friends who supported each other and arranged occasional evenings out together.

Mary Stott, OBE (1907–2002)

Mary Stott was an influential figure in the women's liberation movement. She was born in Leicester on 18 July 1907 to a family of journalists. After an education at Wyggeston Grammar School in Leicester, she joined the *Leicester Mail* where she learned about newspaper production as well as doing some reporting. When she was told to edit the woman's page she was bitterly disappointed, as she felt it marked the end of her career as a 'proper' journalist.

After leaving the *Leicester Mail* she worked first for the *Bolton Evening News* and then the Co-operative Press. During this time she married and had a daughter, Catherine (who also became a journalist). In spite of being a wife and mother, Mary continued working. In 1945 she took a job as sub-editor of the *Manchester Evening News*, becoming the first woman news sub-editor. Although she claimed that she met with little sex-discrimination and was promoted to assistant chief sub-editor, she was never allowed to take the chief sub-editor's place in his absence, as his replacement had to be a man.

In 1957, after seven years in semi-retirement, she accepted a job editing the women's page of the *Manchester Guardian*. Although she was initially reluctant to leave what she considered 'real' journalism for the women's pages, she remained as editor until 1972, by which time she had created a respected platform for women's issues. She broke away from the more conventional women's page, which traditionally dealt with domestic matters, and invited her readers to consider the broader issues of the day. Under her editorship, the page became a vehicle for a number of campaigns. The National Housewives Register, the Pre-School Playground Association and the National Association for the Welfare of Children in Hospital were among the groups that were founded as a result of issues brought up in her pages.

Mary Stott was also unusual in the amount of space she gave to unsolicited material from amateur writers. It was her way of giving a voice to her readers. She also gave space to a number of talented women writers. Through her pages women became aware of alternative ways of thinking and of living. Although she was not a strident feminist she was an active campaigner outside the pages of the *Guardian*, and served on a number of committees. In 1973 she led a march to Downing Street for Women in Media but in an echo of the days of the suffragette deputations, the Prime Minister, Ted Heath, refused to meet them. Instead they were allowed to deliver a written message. In 1975, she was made an OBE. Although she stopped working as women's editor in 1972, she did not retire: she continued to write a column for the page, and wrote several books between 1973 and 1987. In her obituary in the *Guardian*, Lena Jeger described her as 'one of the great campaigning journalists of the twentieth century'. She died on 16 September 2002.

Unlike Myra, Maureen Nicol, who moved to a new area where she knew no one, felt isolated and bored during the day with only a baby and a toddler for company. In 1960, she wrote to the *Guardian* in response to an article about stay-at-home wives. Her letter, which was published by Mary Stott (see profile), suggested that 'housebound wives with ... a desire to remain individuals could form a national register'. She was surprised by the response to her letter as hundreds of women wrote to her wanting to join her organisation. That was the start of the National Housewives Register which provided women with names of similarly minded women in their locality. Women then formed their own local groups which organised discussion groups, baby-sitting rotas and other projects to keep them active and in touch with the outside world.

Women in the House of Commons

Although they had been eligible to become MPs since 1918, until recent years the number of women elected to Parliament was small. At the start of the 1960s there were only 25 women MPs and although this number increased to 28 in 1964, it went down again at the following election. The small number of women in the House of Commons did not reflect a lack of interest in politics: they were very active behind the scenes in the political parties and several thousand were councillors in local government.

Part of the reason why so few became MPs lay in the way that the political parties treated women candidates. According to a table in Martin Pugh's book, *Women and the Women's Movement in Britain*, 249 women stood in parliamentary elections during the 1950s but only 25 of them were given safe seats to contest. The overwhelming majority, 175, were put in unwinnable constituencies. In addition, the reluctance of parties at constituency levels to accept women candidates remained a barrier for many decades and was one of the reasons why the Labour Party introduced positive discrimination in the 1990s.

The late night sittings of Parliament were another reason why few women considered becoming MPs. In June 1964 the *Sunday Times Magazine* published an article on female MPs which showed the difficulty faced by those with family responsibilities. Judith Hart, one of the few with school-age children, was fortunate enough to have a cook to prepare her family's evening meal. When there were late night sittings she would go home at 7 p.m. to see her children and then return to the House of Commons. Not all women would be in a position to follow her example, either because they could not afford paid help or because their family home was too far away. It is interesting that, according to the article, of the 25 women MPs at the time only 11 were married and only 4 had school-age children.

The article also claimed that the biggest disadvantage a female MP faced was that she could never have a wife. It was making a serious point. In the 1960s, many constituencies preferred to have married men as candidates as in most cases it meant that his wife came as part of the package. A wife was considered an asset to the constituency, as she could host parties and receptions. She was also expected to field telephone calls and deal with many constituency problems, much in the way that a vicar's wife was considered to be at the beck and call of his parishioners. A husband, however supportive, would be expected to have a job and so be unable to help his MP wife in the same way.

Although the 1964 election saw only a small increase in the number of women MPs, the new Prime Minister, Harold Wilson, was more prepared to promote them than any of his predecessors had been, and included several in his cabinet. In the past, the few women Cabinet Ministers had been placed in areas associated with social welfare, but Barbara Castle (see also p. 142), after a spell in Overseas Development, was put in charge of Transport, where she was vilified by some for introducing the breathalyser. She was then moved to Employment where she won the battle to have equal pay included in the Government's incomes policy.

In the 1960s there were a number of laws which affected women's rights. As well as the change in the abortion law discussed above, from 1964 married women were allowed to keep half of any money they saved out of their housekeeping allowances. In 1967, they were given similar rights to the marital home as their husbands. Although Barbara Castle, with the backing of other women MPs, was responsible for making equal pay part of government policy, it is not clear whether these laws were the direct result of pressure from women MPs.

The reform of the divorce law in 1969, however, created a great deal of controversy. Before 1969 only the 'innocent party' in a marriage could sue for divorce, and an 'innocent' wife could refuse to a divorce her husband even if he had left home and was living with another woman. Some women did this because of their religious beliefs or from a mistaken conviction that, given time, their husbands would return. Some were reluctant to become a divorcee at a time when society frowned on them whether or not they were the 'innocent party'. A few refused out of spite, denying the 'other woman' her chance of marriage. In some cases the 'innocent party' was a husband but, in general, men were more likely to divorce an unfaithful wife.

The 1969 change in the law made the 'irretrievable breakdown' of a marriage the only cause for divorce. As a result a husband was free to divorce his wife, even if he was the 'guilty party', and remarry if he wished. This angered many 'innocent' wives and those who saw it as a threat to marriage. The MP, Dr Edith Summerskill, opposed the change and referred to the new law as a 'Casanova's charter'. Women who had been forced by the social climate of the time to pose as wives welcomed the change, as they could marry and legitimise their children.

What permissive society?

Whether or not women experienced the 'permissive society' depended very much on where they lived and what circles they moved in. For the most part, the 'swinging sixties' phenomenon took place in London and in a few bohemian communities. It also became more widespread as the decade wore on. What most people associate with the 1960s — the drugs, free love and the widespread use of the pill — did not come about until the second half of the decade and, again, the impact was limited. When asked about the 'swinging sixties', Myra Noble said that they did not reach Presbyterian Scotland. When Maureen Pond was in the WRAF

The Clean up TV Campaign

For some people, the existence of the 'permissive society' was not only real, it was a serious threat to the country. In 1964, in response to what she saw as a concerted attempt to undermine the morals of the country by television broadcasters, Mrs Mary Whitehouse, a former schoolteacher, founded the Clean up TV Campaign. She clearly believed in taking her objections to the top, and wrote regularly to the Postmaster General, the Prime Minister and the Queen. A note in a file in the National Archives (HO 256/719) records that, up to 19 September 1967, she had sent a total of 57 letters and 8 telegrams.

One of those telegrams, addressed to the Prime Minister, is in the file. It must have been sent soon after the end of an episode of *Till Death Do Us Part*, a programme in which the character Alf Garnett rarely said a sentence without the word 'bloody' in it. The telegram read, 'someone, somewhere has to take responsibility'. The file also contains several letters objecting to the same programme. Her main objection, apart from the swearing, was that the programme was shown at 7.30 p.m., early enough for children to be watching. However, given her right-wing views, it is likely that she would have found some of the liberal and socialist views put forward by the characters played by Tony Booth and Una Stubbs just as objectionable.

Another of her letters gives some support to the idea that the 'swinging sixties' was largely a London phenomenon. She referred to 'the repugnance which exists in the provinces for much of what has come to be known as "Swinging London"', and blamed the BBC for moulding public opinion rather than reflecting it. She also felt that the BBC was giving free publicity to the 'hippie' way of life and encouraging the use of drugs. She asked the Government to control the BBC programmers while at the same time denying that she wanted censorship. There was some support for her views and in one letter she referred to a deputation to present over 300,000 signatures supporting her campaign.

The National Viewer's and Listener's Association, which grew out of the Clean up TV Campaign, seemed to feel that they were having some influence on the content of television programmes. In a bulletin, dated January 1967, they claimed that there was less sex and violence on television as a result of their campaigning. They warned, however, that the attack on morals and an attempt to swing public opinion behind 'permissive reforms' was continuing, though it was more subtle.

during the 1960s, women were warned off sex by films and lectures about the dangers of venereal disease, but they received no advice about birth control.

Even in London in the early 1960s many girls staying in the city's hostels had to be back by 11 p.m. or else they were locked out. Men were strictly forbidden from entering the premises and one woman remembers that in her nurses' home even fathers had to have special permission before they could take their daughters' suitcases up to their rooms. A Catholic hostel in Victoria was even stricter: girls were forbidden to dance in any of the ground floor rooms in case they were seen by passing men. Some girls avoided the rule to be in early by staying out until morning. This, however, could be quite innocent. There were many all-night cafes in central London where girls could sit in safety until they could get back into their hostels.

Even in the late 1960s, strictness was the norm in the Middlesborough nurses' home where Sue Hanson (later Griffiths) stayed. Nurses had to be in by 9 p.m. but, once a week, they were allowed a late pass until 10 p.m. If they wanted to stay out any later, they got the third degree from the sister who once a month could grant a pass until midnight, provided she was satisfied with their reason. Many nurses, however, got round the rules by climbing out of a window. Once when Sue did this she slipped and broke her wrist. The next day she was hauled before Matron who duly wrote to her parents. It is possibly a measure of the change in the times that Sue's parents found the incident amusing.

In complete contrast, Carol Allen, who came from Liverpool, recalled the tremendous sense of freedom, the wild parties and the excitement of the period. When she first moved to London she found that anyone who came from Liverpool was treated as royalty. When people discovered that she knew Paul McCartney's brother she was invited to a number of parties. Although she had had elocution lessons, she recalled practising a Liverpool accent before going out. Most of all she remembered the joy of throwing off convention and simply enjoying herself. She felt that women at that time were keen to experience the freedom flaunted by icons like Marianne Faithfull. In her circle, sex was no longer bad or sinful, but fun. However, she did not believe that sexual freedom in the 1960s was simply a result of the pill: she felt that the more relaxed attitude came from drugs that loosened inhibitions and made people feel that anything was possible.

While this attitude was not widespread, attitudes to pre-marital sex were slowly changing. In *Family Planning Today*, published in 1963, Dr Mary Pollock acknowledged that some young people were 'having intercourse' without being engaged or married, and wrote that whether it was right or wrong was for them to decide. Her warnings about the consequences indicate that she did not approve, but she attempted to avoid making moral judgements, choosing instead to emphasise the importance of using contraceptives in order to avoid an unwanted pregnancy.

In July 1963, Dr Henderson, the Principal Medical Officer to the Ministry of Education, stirred controversy when he told a small audience of university and college lectures and teachers that he did not believe a young couple who had sexual intercourse before their marriage were immoral. In a press notice which is in the National Archives file ED 50/862, the Ministry of Education was at pains to point out that Dr Henderson's views were his own and that he was not telling teachers what to teach young people. However it is interesting to note that he is anxious to stress he does not condone promiscuity. While his views would have

From left: Christine Keeler, David Bailey, Penelope Tree and Marianne Faithfull, all 1960s icons. This photograph taken in 1969, only a year after the photograph on p.118, illustrates the difference between London fashions and those outside the capital.

reflected those of many young people, many of the older generation would have disagreed with him.

Certainly in the early 1960s the double standard still existed and while a promiscuous man was praised as a 'bit of a lad', a woman who slept around was called a number of derogatory names. At one hospital, although it was acceptable to sleep with a steady boyfriend or a fiancé, a girl who slept around was known as 'the hospital bike'. While men queued up for her favours, she was definitely not one that they would take home to mother. Until the late 1960s, many men still wanted to marry virgins or at least they wanted to be the only man their future wife had slept with.

Christabel Pankhurst had believed that once women had the vote and were equal citizens, they would be free from sexual exploitation. She could not have been more wrong. The freedoms of the 1960s resulted in an ever-increasing portrayal of women as sexual objects. In popular films and in television programmes such as the 'Carry On' films and the Benny Hill show, sexual harassment was portrayed as normal and acceptable behaviour. Not only is her name degrading, though at the time many saw it as witty, but the scene in *Goldfinger* where Bond overcomes Pussy Galore is disturbingly akin to rape.

Mary Quant, OBE (1934–)

Ask anyone to think of an image of the 1960s and the chances are that they will picture Twiggy in a Mary Quant dress (see photograph). For many, Mary Quant's geometric designs and straight, short shift dresses epitomise the decade. Her 'Chelsea look' even influenced Paris fashion. She was an innovative designer and broke the fashion rules by using unusual colour combinations and by mixing patterns. She also created fun furs and introduced new fabrics like PVC. Her aim was to produce fun, sexy clothes for young women, which would be very different from the staid fashions worn by their mothers. In 1967, in an interview with the *Guardian*, she claimed that 'good taste is death, vulgarity is life'.

When she started out she cannot have imagined how successful she and her designs would be. Born in London in 1934, she enrolled at Goldsmith's College of Art after leaving school. Soon after, even though she had no experience of selling clothes, she decided to open her own boutique. In 1955, she opened 'Bazaar' on the Kings Road with two friends. She soon became dissatisfied with the clothes available and decided to create and stock her own designs. They were a huge success and her boutique on the King's Road became a fashion mecca and Chelsea the place to be. In 1961, she opened a second 'Bazaar' in Knightsbridge.

In 1966 she was awarded an OBE for putting London on the fashion map. She was a prolific designer and is said to have invented the mini skirt, though that is debatable. She did however create hot pants. Her look, with its flat chest, short skirts and bobbed hair, was reminiscent of the 1920s, though her use of heavy eyeliner and PVC raincoats was not. Before Mary Quant, fashion designers produced clothes for the wealthy. Although the rich and famous wore her styles, her contribution was to make fashion accessible to ordinary young women.

One of the consequences of the images of sexually 'liberated' women was that some men assumed that any woman was available. In Cumbria, I was warned against wearing 'London' fashions while in the north because the 'men were hungry'. The warning was well meant. In the way that some blamed the 1920s 'flappers' for causing men's infidelity, so mini-skirted women were blamed for rape. It was felt by many men, including a few judges, that women who wore 'provocative' clothing were 'asking for it'. The slow realisation that the new sexual freedom was more exploitative than liberating was an important feature of the women's liberation movement and would find its voice in the next decade.

Mary Quant among models wearing her footwear in 1967. Such poses would have been unthinkable a decade earlier when women were expected to be elegant and decorous.

Feminists or free spirits?

I myself have never been able to find out precisely what feminism is:
I only know that people call me a feminist whenever I express sentiments that
differentiate me from a doormat or a prostitute.

REBECCA WEST, 1913

The 1970s was a turbulent decade, characterised by political upheavals and a growing restlessness in the population. There were four Prime Ministers and as many elections, and the period saw a great deal of unrest amongst workers which culminated in the 1978–9 'winter of discontent'. Women too were affected by the upheavals and the 1970s saw the growth of the women's liberation movement, legislation favourable to women and, in 1975, the unexpected election of Margaret Thatcher as leader of the Conservative Party. By the end of the decade, 51 years after women first won equal voting rights with men, Britain had its first woman Prime Minister.

In keeping with the changing mood of the times there were three contrasting images of women in the 1970s. The first, which appeared towards the end of the 1960s, was of the free-spirited 'hippie' who, in her drug-induced euphoria, happily ignored society's unwritten rules. Dressed in her caftan, her long hair flowing, the 1970s 'free spirit' practised free love and preached peace and togetherness as she experimented with communal living. The second was of the dungaree clad, Doc Marten booted, feminist. The feminist or 'women's libber' received a bad press in much the same way as the suffragettes had at the start of the century. Whatever the evidence to the contrary, she was portrayed as an ugly, man-hating and sexually frustrated spinster or lesbian. The third image, which appeared only at the end of the decade, was of the anarchic and aggressive punk. Sexy without being feminine, she redefined what it was to be a woman.

Nice girls do – the real sexual revolution

Although few women in the 1970s practised free love, the decade did see a widespread relaxation in sexual morals. For centuries women had been warned of the consequences of losing their virginity before marriage. 'Nice girls don't' was the mantra that even women in the 1960s were used to hearing. In 1963, *Woman's Own* advised a 34-year-old reader to think twice before losing her virginity as this would ruin her reputation and her chances of marriage. A man, she was warned, 'will not take on the responsibilities of marriage if he can have its privileges for free'. Even as late as 1967 *Woman's Weekly* was advising its readers not to 'anticipate marriage'. By the early 1970s, however, the message was very different. In 1971, the women's magazine *Vanity Fair* produced a booklet entitled *Nice Girls Do*. Readers were left in no doubt as to the meaning, as it was subtitled '*Vanity Fair*'s guide to the new sexual etiquette'.

As well as the usual material on grooming, clothes and make-up, the booklet dealt with issues of contraception and unwanted pregnancies. It also gave advice about living together and covered the best way to conduct office affairs. It even discussed the 'etiquette' of adultery, reminding married women about to embark on an affair to be discreet. Its advice that single women should to go a Family Planning Clinic reflects the change in policy which allowed the clinics to give contraceptive advice to any woman, irrespective of her marital status, providing she was at least sixteen.

During the 1970s young couples were not only sleeping together, an increasing number were choosing to live together, especially in cities and in universities. Such behaviour, however, was not acceptable to all parents. At Lancaster University in the mid 1970s one girl was distraught when her father refused to support her

OPPOSITE
A women's liberation march in 1971: London feminists carried a cross decorated with a female torso and objects from domestic life. They were campaigning for equal pay and expanded rights and opportunities for women. Compare this with the more sedate, but no less determined, protest in the 1950s on p.112.

through university after he discovered that she was sleeping with her boyfriend. The reason he gave was that he was not prepared to support another man's mistress. His attitude, though harsh and archaic, might possibly have been understandable had his daughter been the kept mistress of a wealthy older man, but her boyfriend was a young fellow student.

Vanity Fair's booklet also provided a reminder that, as in the 1960s, attitudes outside the big cities were less permissive. In its advice on cohabiting it pointed out that landlords in small towns and in rural areas were unlikely to let accommodation to a couple unless they were married or about to be married. However, although *Vanity Fair* advised discretion, its matter of fact tone when discussing cohabitation suggests that living together was becoming more common. Martin Pugh supports this view in *Women and the Women's Movement in Britain*, where he states that the number of marriages declined after 1972.

A feature of the more liberal attitudes of the 1970s was the increase in the number of single women who, finding themselves pregnant, not only rejected a shotgun marriage but also refused to give up their child for adoption. The option of keeping an illegitimate child had been open to single women before but it was rarely taken because of society's strong disapproval of both mother and child — even in the 1960s an illegitimate child was seen as the product of sin. The few that kept their child before the mid 1970s were among the fortunate ones who either had the support of their families or else could work and care for their child alone.

Before the 1976 Adoption Act, single mothers, especially those sent to homes for unmarried mothers, came under a great deal of pressure to give up their children for adoption. Although financial assistance had been available to single mothers since 1948, the majority of them were unaware of these benefits. According to an article in the *Observer* in July 2000 about women who were forced to give up their children, women in homes for unmarried mothers were not told about the assistance available to them. Instead, they were warned of the perils of keeping their children. Lorraine Legate, who was fifteen when she became pregnant in 1972, was told that she would end up on the streets, her baby would be taken away and she would not be allowed to have any more children if she tried to keep the child. Some women who were forced to give up their children married and fell pregnant soon after in an attempt to assuage their terrible sense of loss.

The 1970s sexual revolution was not confined to the young, single and heterosexual. Behind the lace curtains of suburbia, the middle classes experimented with wife swapping and the idea of open marriages, though whether this was as widespread as popular belief suggests is doubtful. The relaxation in the law concerning homosexuality in 1967 and the formation of the Gay Liberation Front in 1970 also brought lesbianism out into the open. It is interesting to note, however,

A husband and wife wearing the unisex clothes and hairstyles of the 1970s. Although the majority rejected the more extreme styles of the decade, even older women began to wear trousers, and trouser suits became popular. Although some rejected make-up and nail varnish they were still widely used. Unisex for men meant growing their hair and wearing brighter colours, but while women were adopting male styles of clothing there were no David Beckham style sarongs or nail varnish for the 1970s man.

that for all its liberal views, the *Vanity Fair* booklet did not broach the topic of lesbian relationships.

Women's liberation

Looked at objectively, there seems no reason why women should reject the idea of 'women's liberation' as few of them would argue that they should be anything but free. Similarly it is difficult to see why they would shy away from the description 'feminist' (the *Oxford Dictionary* defines feminism as 'advocacy of women's rights on the grounds of equality of the sexes') – yet many did. Much of their reluctance seemed to stem from their perception of a 'women's libber' or feminist as someone who rejected her femininity and, as a result, was somehow less of a woman. Many women, especially in the early 1970s, seemed confused and slightly hostile to the idea of 'women's lib'. In 1971, in an attempt to cut through prejudice towards the movement, *Vanity Fair* devoted a page of its booklet on modern etiquette to the subject.

Under the heading 'Co-existing with Women's Lib', *Vanity Fair* told its readers that the women's liberation movement deserved serious attention.

Although it took a light-hearted approach to the subject, as though expecting some of its readers to be hostile, it asked them not to dismiss the movement from a position of ignorance. It described the movement as being 'many-splendoured' and 'multi-splintered' and suggested that readers should find out more by joining a consciousness-raising group and reading feminist literature. The fact that *Vanity Fair* felt it necessary to tackle the topic, however gently, suggests that by 1971 it was a subject too large to ignore. The magazine's reference to the need to co-exist with 'our militant sisters', however, indicates that many of its readers did not relate to the movement. When it urged readers not to ridicule the movement it was clear that it wanted them to think beyond the question of whether or not to wear a bra.

One widespread misconception, which put many women off the movement, was that it was against women making themselves attractive to the opposite sex. This view was reinforced when feminists protested against the 1970 Miss World contest (see photograph), claiming that it was demeaning for women to be inspected and judged on their physical attributes like cattle in a market. Taking a leaf out of the suffragettes' book, some women took direct action and disrupted the contest by throwing flour and stink bombs and chanting 'we're not beautiful, we're not ugly, we're angry'. The point that many people missed, women included, was that the feminists did not set out to be killjoys, but had a serious point to make. They were objecting to a culture in which women were treated as having only a domestic or decorative function. As Women in Media (see p. 143) noted, in a culture where women were not taken seriously it was difficult for them to get work in anything other than supporting roles.

For all the scorn and ridicule poured on them at the time, feminists in Britain raised issues that concerned most if not all women. At the first women's liberation conference in 1970 they demanded equal pay; equal education and opportunity; twenty-four hour nurseries; and free contraception and abortion on demand. While not all would agree with abortion on demand, few if any women today would reject equal pay or equal opportunities or object too strongly to free contraception. The demand for twenty-four hour nurseries, though seen by some as anti-family and a way for mothers to abdicate their responsibilities, was intended to provide safe child-care for women who worked shifts. Later demands included the right to financial and legal independence.

While the women's liberation conferences and the marches and demon-strations kept feminist demands in the public eye, behind the scenes there were countless small groups working to effect change. Women not only joined consciousness-raising groups where they discussed their position in society; many helped to set up women's centres and refuges. They also went out into their

One target for women's
liberation protesters was the
1970 Miss World Competition.
This picture shows the winner,
Jennifer Horsten of Grenada.

locality and campaigned on a number of issues, including equal pay and
opportunities, and for the provision of nurseries.

It is difficult to estimate the numbers that were active in the Women's
Liberation movement of the 1970s, as it was not a membership-based organisation.
Neither was it a movement of women with the same set of political beliefs. As
Vanity Fair put it, the movement was a multi-splintered thing and feminists came
in all shapes and sizes and shades of political opinion. While the liberal and
socialist feminists were prepared to work with men, the more radical or
revolutionary feminists rejected them. A few women stood by the slogan 'all men
are rapists' and went so far as to say that women should cut themselves off from

Shrews, viragos and spare ribs

Although feminists have often been accused of lacking a sense of humour, some of the titles of their publications, such as *Shrew* and *Spare Rib*, suggest otherwise. Just as the suffragettes produced their own newspapers and pamphlets to publicise their views, a number of feminist magazines were published during the 1970s to spread the message of women's liberation. Many of them were short-lived, but the glossy *Spare Rib* launched in 1972 was the first to be commercially successful.

The following year the publisher Virago's first official board meeting took place. Virago was the brainchild of Carmen Callil who wanted to create a mass-market publisher for women. It published many of the leading feminist thinkers and many books by women writers which were long out of print, including Mrs Pankhurst's *My Own Story*. It also published women's history and from the 1980s it expanded its list to include books by and about British Black and Asian women.

the male sex altogether. They claimed that men were the enemy and argued that it was a woman's political duty to become a lesbian. Unfortunately it was these views that put some women off identifying with feminism.

Though the number of active feminists was only a small percentage of the female population, their ideas, directly or otherwise, did influence the lives of ordinary women, many of whose expectations changed over the decade. One woman, a housewife and mother, said that when she married in the early 1960s wives were expected to agree with their husband's views. She followed this practice until some time in the 1970s when, although never a feminist, she found herself voicing her own opinions and shocking her husband by disagreeing with his.

Although there were many different women's groups around the country, it was not necessary to belong to one in order to be a feminist. Any woman who thought she was the equal of a man and showed that she expected to be treated accordingly could be described as a feminist in the broadest sense of the word. Even Margaret Thatcher, for all her rejection of the women's liberation movement, was a feminist in that sense: by becoming Prime Minister she rejected the sexual stereotyping that limited the type of work that women could do. It is interesting that many women when discussing an injustice such as equal pay resort to the phrase 'I'm not a feminist but ...'

Equal Pay

Although some women had won equal pay in the 1950s (see p. 112) little progress was made in extending it to others until Barbara Castle (see profile, p. 142) became Employment Minister. In 1968 she intervened in a strike by women machinists at the Ford factory in Dagenham, who were protesting at being graded as unskilled workers, even though they were only employed if they passed a proficiency test. She persuaded them to accept a pay rise without upgrading and promised to introduce equal pay legislation. She kept her word and in 1970 the Equal Pay Act was passed. A file in the National Archives (PREM 13/3554), however, suggests that the Government had an additional motive for introducing equal pay legislation, as there is reference to bringing the UK into line with the countries of the European Economic Community.

The file also gives an insight into the difficulties that Barbara Castle faced in 1969 while discussing the proposed legislation with the employers and unions. Some objected to legislation, arguing that equal pay should be a matter for negotiation, but, no doubt with the Ford machinists strike in mind, she argued that a phased programme of increases would be better for the employers than having to face widespread industrial unrest. She also had to deal with arguments over timing, as the Trades Union Congress (TUC) wanted equal pay implemented within two years of an Act whereas the Confederation of British Industry (CBI) argued for at least a seven year delay.

The most difficult part of the negotiations, however, centred on how equal pay would be applied. Discussions about wording included 'equal pay for equal work' and 'equal pay for the same work'. In the event, the 1970 Equal Pay Act was far from perfect as it applied essentially to work which was the same as, or broadly similar to, that of a man. The Act did try to include women employed in jobs not done by men, by allowing equal pay if a job evaluation could show a woman's job had equal value to one done by a man, but it did not make such job evaluations compulsory.

Despite the Act including sick pay and holiday entitlements, it proved to be a disappointment: many employers reorganised their workplaces during the five years before it was implemented to avoid paying women more. One woman, who had expected a large rise when she took over her section head's job on his promotion, was disappointed by her new pay rate. She queried the amount but was

Baroness Barbara Castle (1910–2002)

Barbara Castle, the first woman to hold three major cabinet posts, was a feisty and passionate politician who never ceased to campaign for what she believed to be social justice. Born in Bradford on 6 October 1910, she was brought up in a radical household where women were treated as equals. She was educated at Bradford Grammar School and at St Hugh's College, Oxford. Some time after leaving university, she moved to London where she joined the Labour Party. In 1937 she became a councillor for St Pancras Borough Council. She was one of the founders of *Tribune*, a left wing weekly, and was involved in the research that led to the Beveridge report, which laid the foundations for the Welfare State.

In 1945, thanks in part to the intervention of the Labour women in Blackburn who had threatened to stop working for the party unless she was added to the short list of candidates, she was elected as MP there. Within a short space of time she was promoted but she had to wait until the Labour government was elected in 1964 before taking cabinet office. After a spell as Overseas Minister she was appointed Minister for Transport. While at Transport, she introduced the 70 m.p.h. speed limit, the breathalyser, and the compulsory wearing of seat-belts. Although these measures have since saved innumerable lives, at the time they were highly unpopular and she met with a great deal of hostility and abuse, much of it because she was a woman and a non-driver.

Her next appointment was as Employment Minister where, if some of the articles published since her death are to believed, she is remembered more for her divisive and unsuccessful policy to curb wildcat strikes than for her achievement in pushing through the 1970 Equal Pay Act. When Labour returned to power in 1974 she was put in charge of social security, where she linked pension rises to earnings. When James Callaghan became Prime Minister in 1976 he sacked her because of her age. She stayed on the back benches until 1979, but instead of retiring gracefully (she was 69) she stood for and was elected to the European Parliament.

After serving as an MEP for ten years, she accepted a seat in the House of Lords where for the next thirteen years she made justice for pensioners her main platform. She did not relax or retire when New Labour was elected in 1997 but continued to fight for her socialist beliefs. Her biggest disappointment was that New Labour failed to restore the link between earnings and pensions, which had been removed by the Conservative party during their time in office. She died on 3 May 2002.

told that she was not doing the same job as her predecessor. When she checked her new job description she found that, although the job title had changed, there were only minor differences from her predecessor's job specification. She felt unable to object further, as she was met with a 'take it or leave it' attitude. For the majority of women, however, equal pay was not even an issue, as they did not do the same work as men and few employers made any attempt to set up job evaluation schemes.

Although the Equal Pay Act did little for the majority of women, its existence, together with the influence of the women's movement, gave a number of them the confidence to protest against low pay. In August 1972, *The Times* reported on the strike organised by the Cleaners' Action Group who were campaigning for better pay and conditions for all cleaners, but especially for night workers who were among the most exploited. At the time of the report the cleaners were picketing the Ministry of Defence. Their leader, May Hobbs, claimed that she had more respect for the Mafia because they, unlike the Government, did not exploit their cleaners.

The file (PREM 13/3554) also records that there was an attempt to use the equal pay legislation to remove restrictions on women's working hours, especially those that prevented them from working night shifts. The unions resisted any changes, claiming that the restrictions were discrimination in favour of women. One of the TUC representatives argued that 'women were biologically different and were liable to exploitation'. Barbara Castle, however, argued that while women should not be forced to work night shifts they should not be forbidden from doing so. She pointed out that if all women faced the same restrictions in working hours she, for one, would not be able to do her job.

Equal Opportunities

When the 1919 Sex Disqualification (Removal) Act (see p. 53) gave women the right to enter a number of professions previously closed to them, they must have believed that the battle to end discrimination was won. Yet, as a document from Women in Media in the National Archives file HO 245/737 shows, more than half a century later discrimination was still rife. The document, which was sent to the Committee for the Future of Broadcasting in January 1975, dealt with the women's concerns over career opportunities, working conditions, and the way women were portrayed on radio and television.

One cause for concern was the number of women graduates who were recruited as secretaries with the promise of an eventual career in broadcasting which rarely materialised. As Penelope Lively had observed in the 1950s (see also p. 111),

Open University

The Open University (OU), which took its first students in 1971, was founded for those who, for whatever reason, had missed out on a university education. Women were quick to take advantage of this opportunity and from the start the majority of OU students has been women. Its system of distance learning, in which students receive packages of course materials supplemented by television and radio programmes, proved ideal for women with family responsibilities. Although students communicated with their tutors by post, they were given a taste of university life at summer schools. These were held in university campuses where they attended lectures, seminars and tutorials and mixed with other students. The OU changed many women's lives, mine included: I enjoyed the summer school experience so much that I gave up my job to become a full-time student at Lancaster University.

the secretarial route was never suggested to male graduates. Women in Media also complained that in the period since 1959, only three women (compared to 44 men) had been sent on production training schemes and that very few women attended the BBC's senior management courses. They noted as well that women very rarely held technical positions and that, while they were often employed as assistants, they never got the top jobs. The document also records that Women in Media objected to the way that women were either portrayed as home-obsessed housewives or as young females there to entertain. They wanted women employed as newscasters and as presenters of serious programmes.

Women in Media was only one of the many groups campaigning for equal opportunities and an end to discrimination against women. Support also came from sympathetic MPs and on two separate occasions a private member's bill to end discrimination on the grounds of sex was put forward. Neither was successful as the tactic of talking them out, familiar from the days of the suffragettes (see p. 18), was used to prevent the bills from becoming law. However, the 1975 Sex Discrimination Act was passed soon after the Labour party returned to power in 1974.

The Act covered housing, employment, training and the provision of goods and services, and it also established the Equal Opportunities Commission (EOC). The EOC's role was to promote equal opportunities and fight cases of discrimination. There were complaints that it was ineffective but it had some success. In one case it managed to convince the Civil Service that its age limit of 28 for entry to its executive grade discriminated against women who stayed at home to raise a family, as they were too old to enter the grade on their return to work. As a result the age limit was raised to 45.

One woman who took full advantage of the Sex Discrimination Act was Bella Keyzer (see p. 99) who had been forced to leave her job as a welder at the end of the Second World War. Since then, although she knew that as a woman she would not be taken on, she had applied for a number of welding jobs, using her initials rather than her full name. She was often called for an interview but once employers saw she was a woman they refused to employ her even though she was highly qualified. As soon as the Act was passed she applied again to became a welder and this time was accepted. Although she had applied for the job because she enjoyed welding, she benefited financially from the change. With her victory, her wages rose from £27 a week to the welder's rate of £73.

The 1975 Act also made it easier for women to get financial credit. Although by the 1950s banks were advertising the benefits of a bank account in women's magazines, it was extremely difficult for a woman to obtain credit or a mortgage without a male guarantor. Before the Act, Carol McCormick Smith had been forced to obtain her ex-husband's signature in order to get a television set; fortunately they had remained on good terms. Even after the Act was passed it took a while for some men to come to terms with its implications. In her article, 'The Woman's Hour', which is on the BBC website, Jenni Murray, presenter of the radio programme of the same name, wrote that when she applied for a mortgage in 1976, she was told that she needed her father's signature. It was only after she cited the Sex Discrimination Act that the building society manager backed down, 'for fear of legal action!'.

One of the most important aspects of the Act was the way that it raised awareness of discrimination. Its effect was even felt among the young. In May 1978, the *Times Educational Supplement* reported on the case of seven 13-year-olds who, when they were refused permission to take a car maintenance class, threatened to take their grievance to the Equal Opportunities Commission. The head of their comprehensive school in Maidenhead claimed that he had made the decision to exclude the girls from the oversubscribed class because 'on a Sunday morning in Maidenhead you will find the man under the car and the woman looking after the baby'. Once the head was made aware of the implications of the law he backed down, but complained that he had had to deprive other children of four periods of craft in order to accommodate the girls.

As in the example above, the threat of taking a case to the EOC was often enough to effect a desired change in schools. In another mixed comprehensive, a male science teacher was forced to change his end of term reports after a female teacher complained about his repeated assertions that physics was a boy's subject. Although his thinking did not change, he was no longer allowed to air his views in the school. His attitude was not uncommon among male teachers so it is hardly surprising that few girls in the past succeeded in the sciences.

One area where the act failed to remedy injustice was in the realms of pensions and income tax. Resentment in this area led to the 'Why be a wife? campaign'. As early as the 1920s, Marie Stopes (see profile, p. 62) had complained that the law favoured those who lived in sin by taxing married couples as one person. On one occasion, after I had overpaid income tax, my husband received a letter informing him that he was due a tax refund. Although the letter asked him to state the name he wanted on the cheque, giving him the opportunity to give mine, which he did, at no point did the Inland Revenue write and tell me about the overpayment. No doubt many other men in the same situation also gave the tax refund to their wives but it is likely that a number did not.

Although an increasing number of women were working after they had children some employers continued to force women to leave work once they became pregnant. The 1975 Employment Protection Act made this illegal: it also gave women the right to six weeks' paid maternity leave and extended unpaid leave to 29 weeks. This legislation was a far cry from the attitudes of earlier governments which had actively discouraged mothers of young children from going out to work.

Women take action

A remarkable feature of the 1970s was the way that women, whether directly influenced by the women's movement or not, were taking matters into their own hands instead of leaving things to the institutions or to the politicians. The creation of refuges for battered wives is a prime example. In 1971 the first refuge was opened in Chiswick, West London, by Erin Pizzey (see profile). The refuge not only provided a place of safety for women, it also brought out into the open the issue of domestic violence, which until then had been ignored. Erin's policy that no woman should be turned away from the refuge, however overcrowded it became, brought her trouble from the local council, but at the same time it created valuable publicity for the cause.

A file in the National Archives (HLG 118/1790) contains documents which reveal some of the attitudes in the 1970s towards domestic violence. Material from the Citizens Advice Bureaux (CAB) gives several examples of cases where police had refused to act against a husband even when they had the evidence of a bruised and bloodied woman. In one case a large and violent man beat his wife badly enough to put her in hospital, but the police, who were outside the house at the time, only helped the woman once she managed to open the door. Police claimed

Erin Pizzey (1939–)

Erin Pizzey, who opened Britain's first refuge for battered women in Chiswick in 1971, was born in China in 1939, the daughter of a British diplomat. She travelled widely until she was old enough to be sent to England to be educated. She had an unhappy childhood and left home at 17, soon after her mother's death. In 1961 she married John Pizzey and had a son and daughter. The opening of her refuge for battered women in Chiswick brought the subject of domestic violence out into the open for the first time. As well as working directly with the battered women and their children, she wrote books on the subject and appeared on television to publicise the problem.

Although initially she won a great deal of respect for her work at the Chiswick refuge, she caused controversy and made many enemies with her later views. She accepted that many women genuinely wanted to leave violent husbands or partners and did so when they were given the chance, but she believed that a large number of battered women were addicted to violence. Such women, she believed, would always return to a man who beat them. To support her views she pointed to the number of women who left the refuge to return to their violent partners time and again. In some cases she claimed that they returned home knowing that they were likely to be killed, and in some cases they were. She argued that many children brought up in violent homes sought to recreate the violence of their childhood because it brought them a perverse kind of pleasure.

Her views outraged many women, not only the radical feminists who held the more extreme view that men were the enemy and that 'all men were rapists'. Even feminists who were happy to work alongside men were perturbed by her comments as they sounded too much like the excuses given by violent men that their women enjoyed being beaten. Her views must have reinforced the negative image that many battered women had of themselves and made it more difficult for them to seek help.

In 1974 she published *Scream Quietly or the Neighbours Will Hear*. After 1979 she extended her work to cover general family violence. She divorced in 1979 and in 1980 married Jeffrey Shapiro with whom she wrote *Prone to Violence* (1982). She published a memoir, *Infernal Child*, in 1978.

that it was outside their jurisdiction to interfere in domestic disputes inside the house. It was clear that domestic violence was not taken seriously: one violent and drunken husband who had been smashing things up was told by the police to 'be a good chap and go to bed'.

Much of the complacency towards domestic violence stemmed from the perception held in some quarters that wife beating was acceptable and that women even enjoyed being beaten. Jack Ashley MP claimed that some men regarded wife beating as a perk of marriage, while others blamed the woman's provocation. Cases referred to in the file show that domestic violence was not confined to the lower classes, as many people believed. In one case, a top executive in Berkshire kicked his pregnant wife and one of the twins she was carrying was born dead. It was clear that a violent husband was just as likely to be a 'respectable' manager as an unemployed drunk.

By 1975 many other refuges had opened and the National Women's Aid Federation was formed, though Erin Pizzey did not work within it. After a great deal of pressure from the Federation and with support from sympathetic MPs, the 1976 Domestic Violence Act was passed. Under this Act a woman could apply for a court injunction to protect her from a violent husband or partner.

Also in 1976, feminists opened the first Rape Crisis Centre to help victims of rape. At that time many women were afraid to report rape as they were made to feel as though they were the ones at fault. Police attitudes to rape victims in this period were as bad as, if not worse than, their attitude to battered wives. As Martin Pugh points out, the attitudes of some judges did not help, as men convicted of rape were often let off or treated lightly so as not to harm their careers.

During the 1970s women in Northern Ireland took action against a different kind of violence. In 1976, in response to the killing of three young children in a tragic accident involving the out-of-control car of a dead IRA gunman, the children's aunt, Mairead Corrigan, together with Betty Williams, founded the Northern Ireland Peace Movement (later the Community of Peace People). They organised and led a number of demonstrations and marches in which thousands of women, both Catholic and Protestant, marched together for peace. In spite of hostility and threats from the paramilitaries of both sides, they continued with their work. Their bravery and attempts to bring an end to the sectarian violence won them recognition and they received a number of awards, including the 1976 Nobel Peace Prize.

The spirit of taking action spread into the ethnic communities where women had to contend with racial as well as sexual discrimination. In 1973 the first black women's group was formed in Brixton, and in 1976 the largely female Asian workforce of Grunwick's, led by Jayaben Desai, went on strike for the right to join a union. Two years later, in 1978, the Organisation of Women of Asian and African Descent was formed to fight discrimination, especially in immigration, where women arriving to join their men could be subjected to humiliating virginity tests.

The spirit of optimism which fired many women at beginning of the 1970s, thanks in part to the first national conference of the women's liberation movement and the Equal Pay Act, was by the end of the decade beginning to peter out. Partly as a backlash against the unions, the 1979 general election saw a victory for the Conservative Party and gave Britain its first woman Prime Minister. In theory, with a queen as head of state and a female Prime Minister, the scene should have been set for a radical change for the better in the lives of all women. The reality proved otherwise and life in Britain under Margaret Thatcher was to be very different from the utopia that the early feminists might have envisaged had they ever considered such a possibility.

Having it all?

Today the problem that has no name is how to juggle work, home, love and children.

BETTY FRIEDAN, 1987

Unlike earlier decades, which were marked by generalised images of women such as the 1920s flappers or the 1950s housewife, the last two decades of the century were dominated by the images of two women. Like them or loathe them, during the 1980s and 1990s there was no escaping Margaret Thatcher and Diana, Princess of Wales. Their every move was recorded and they regularly featured in the news, though for very different reasons. In a sense their dominance indicates how far women's lives and expectations had changed since the century began but it also reflected, especially in the case of Diana, the growing cult of celebrity and the importance of image.

Though the contrast between the Prime Minister and the Princess could not have been greater, they both found that their appearance was a matter for public criticism and felt it necessary to submit to 'make-overs'. The Prime Minister's strong image was modified, her hairstyle softened, and her voice toned down and made more soothing and 'feminine'. The young and gauche Lady Diana Spencer was by stages turned into a sophisticated clotheshorse, a supermodel in all but name. Later in the period Hillary Clinton and Cherie Blair, both strong career women, came under the same kind of pressure to glamorise their image once their husbands came to power.

During the period that the Iron Lady, as Mrs Thatcher was nicknamed, dominated the political scene, more women began to move into jobs formerly the preserve of men. With a woman at the helm of state, nothing seemed impossible for the young and ambitious who, with a little help from their 'power' suits, squared their shoulders and prepared to take on the bankers and businessmen in the city and in the boardrooms.

Ironically, although a woman led the country and their party, some male Conservatives did their best to ignore the fact. As party leader, Margaret Thatcher should have been automatically invited to the all-male Conservative Carlton Club, but rather than change the rules to admit women, she was allowed to become a member only after they dubbed her an 'honorary man'. They were not alone in this attitude: she was regularly referred to as either 'the best man in the Government' or 'the only man in the Government'.

By contrast Princess Diana, especially in the early days of her engagement and marriage, epitomised the idealised view of womanhood purveyed by her step-grandmother, the romantic novelist, Barbara Cartland. Had her fairytale romance gone according to plan, once the young Diana had married her prince they would have lived happily ever after. In return for her every need being taken care of all she would have had to do was bear his children and keep her love for him shining brightly.

While it may have been easier, and indeed obligatory, to keep up the pretence of a fairytale marriage early in the century when Barbara Cartland was young, Princess Diana was a woman of the late twentieth century. Her refusal to accept the double standards that prevailed in the past is a measure of how far women's expectations had changed. Unlike countless wives in earlier generations, she was not prepared to turn a blind eye to her husband's infidelity, and she retaliated by taking a lover and making her husband's adultery public. Even after her divorce she refused to fade into the background, and sought to carve out an independent role for herself. It is interesting that after her divorce she grew in confidence and, although always a glamorous figure, she began to shed her 'brainless blonde' image.

OPPOSITE

Margaret Thatcher at a Conservative Party conference in Brighton, 1984. The IRA tried to assassinate her with a bomb earlier in the day.

Princess Diana during a visit to Chicago, 1996.

Her involvement with the Red Cross and the campaign to ban the use of landmines showed that she had a serious side and increased the respect that she had already won by drawing attention to the plight of the homeless and Aids sufferers.

Changing roles

Princess Diana was not alone in refusing to fade into the background. Older women too refused to become invisible once they reached a certain age. Ageism had always affected women more than men, especially in areas of sexuality. Although a man with a younger woman had always been accepted, a relationship between a woman and a younger man was usually frowned upon. Though it is hard to credit now, I knew of a wife who, in the 1950s, lied about her age to hide the fact that she was eighteen months older than her husband. This attitude to age and the fear that their husbands would divorce them in favour of 'newer models' was a reason why some had objected to the change in the divorce law in the 1960s (see p. 128). By the 1980s and 1990s, however, women's new confidence meant that instead of accepting defeat, many older women, divorcees included, started new careers and/or took younger lovers.

As they grew more independent, women became more confident about revealing their age. In Britain sex appeal had always been associated with youth, unlike in France where attractive women of a 'certain age' were considered sexy. As a result there were few leading roles in Britain for older actresses, and mature women were noticeable by their absence on both the large and small screen. From the 1980s this began to change and although the emphasis was still on the young and beautiful there was an increasing number of leading roles for middle-aged women, though not yet for old women.

In the 1980s and 1990s in both film and television Julie Walters, Judi Dench and Helen Mirren were among those who continued to play sexy women 'of a certain age'. Pauline Collins starred in *Shirley Valentine*, which celebrated the rebellion of a middle-aged housewife who went on holiday to Greece and refused to return to her suffocating life in her suburban house. The comedy *Absolutely Fabulous* accustomed the public to the idea that middle-aged women also wanted to have fun. Anita Roddick (see profile, p. 159) spoke out against the cosmetic industry's promise of eternal youth in a jar, and argued that women should accept their wrinkles as a sign that they had lived.

Women also challenged expectations elsewhere and a number of them succeeded in entering what had always been male territory. Baroness Young, who was the only woman to serve even briefly in a Thatcher cabinet, became the first female leader of the House of Lords. Mary Donaldson became the first female Lord Mayor of London in 1983. It is possibly coincidental that, after Mrs Thatcher resigned, a number of other women came to prominence. In 1992, Stella Rimington became the first woman to head MI5 and the first head whose name was made publicly known. In the same year, Betty Boothroyd, MP for West Bromwich West, who had once been a dancer in a chorus line, became the first female Speaker of the House of Commons. In 1995, twenty-nine years after she joined the police force, Pauline Clare was appointed Chief Constable of the Lancashire Constabulary, becoming the first woman to hold that rank.

Black and Asian women too began to make their mark in public life, though the majority still suffered from racial as well as sexual discrimination. Shreela Flather can boast several firsts. She was the first Asian woman councillor and, as Lady Mayor of Windsor and Maidenhead, became the first Asian woman mayor in 1986. She later became the first Asian woman peer. In 1987 Diane Abbott became the first black woman MP when she was elected for Hackney. Ten years later in 1997, Oona King joined her as an MP. In 1989, Valerie Amos headed the Equal Opportunities Commission and in 1997 she became Baroness Amos. (In 2003, she became the first black woman to join the Cabinet when she became minister for Overseas Development.) In 1991, Patricia Scotland, later Baroness Scotland, became the first black woman QC (see profile, p. 164).

Shreela Flather.

Some people found the changing role of women difficult to cope with. Many, especially men, responded to a female Prime Minister by blaming 'that bloody woman' rather than criticising the Government's policies. Over the two decades, however, attitudes began to change as the public became used to seeing women in senior positions. The shift in attitudes was helped by television programmes which portrayed career women in a number of leading roles, though none of these women were black. These programmes may not have been part of a deliberate policy to accustom the public to the changing situation, but perhaps *The Vicar of Dibley*, first shown in 1994, the year in which the Church of England first ordained women priests (see box, p. 154), may have helped get viewers used to the idea.

Other significant programmes were *Prime Suspect*, first shown in 1991, in which Helen Mirren played Detective Chief Inspector Jane Tennison. The programme not only showed a policewoman in a position of

Women priests

When women won the right in 1919 to join a number of professions (see p. 53) both the Stock
Exchange and the Church remained closed to them. Women were finally allowed on the Stock
Exchange in 1973, but, in spite of the 1975 Sex Discrimination Act, the Church of England held out
until 1994 before it ordained women as priests. Among the first group to be ordained, the eldest
was 85-year-old Elsie Baker, who had been a deaconess since 1938. She continued to serve as a
priest until her death in 2003. Although female priests had become common in other countries and
in other denominations such as the Methodists, the practice of ordaining women caused a rift within
the Church of England. Several of its members, men and women, left the Church in protest. Some,
including women, joined the Roman Catholic Church, which remains adamant that it will not ordain
women.

authority but also dealt with the sexism faced by women in the police force.
Although by the 1980s women were being shown as doctors, it was unusual to see
them in the less glamorous branches of medicine. This was remedied by *Silent
Witness*, in which Amanda Burton played the leading role of Professor Sam Ryan,
a forensic pathologist and university lecturer. These programmes helped to change
the perception of women's roles and encouraged young women to raise their
expectations when considering career options.

'Family values' and self-sufficiency

It would be easy, looking at the achievements of those who made the headlines, to
exaggerate the change in women's lives in this period. For the large majority of

them during the 1980s and 1990s bringing up their families remained their first priority. The main difference between their lives and those of women in earlier decades was that more mothers felt obliged to work. A few women worked because they feared an extended break from the workplace would damage their careers, but the majority worked for financial reasons: staying at home was a luxury they could ill afford.

When Margaret Thatcher came to power many women had mixed feelings. On one level they were pleased that a woman had become Prime Minister, but most were aware that her policies were anything but female-friendly. This was reflected in the way that, with the brief exception of Baroness Young, she had no women in her Cabinet. She rejected the notion of 'society', claiming that there was no such thing, and insisted that the best way forward was to go back to Victorian values, with an emphasis on self-reliance and the family. She also believed that she owed nothing to the women's movement and that everything she had achieved had been down to her own efforts.

It is difficult to understand her emphasis on Victorian values given the nature of Victorian society and the way in which women were treated at that time. Although there is no denying that she worked hard to achieve her ambition, she could not have done so in the Victorian period when women had no voice, no vote and were considered to be of little value. It is likely that had she been born a hundred years earlier her father would have said, as Mrs Pankhurst's father had said of her, it was a pity that she had not been born a boy.

In keeping with an idealised view of Victorian family values, but in sharp contrast to the views that she expressed in the 1950s as a young working mother (see p. 113), Mrs Thatcher and some members of her government tried to persuade women to stay at home. This policy might have worked had benefits to mothers been increased. However, by cutting child benefits in 1985 and freezing them in 1987 and 1988, her government ensured that more, not fewer, women would feel compelled to work. Child benefit only survived as a universal benefit thanks to Conservative women's opposition to moves to abolish it. They also successfully killed the idea that child benefits should be paid to men.

As part of the campaign for 'family values' and self-sufficiency, and to reduce the money paid out in benefits, single mothers increasingly came under strong attack during the 1980s. The number of single parent families was growing, as a result of the increase in divorce and because of the decline in the number of marriages. The attack on single mothers proved to be an embarrassment to the Government when Sarah Keyes, the mistress of Cecil Parkinson, one of Mrs Thatcher's favoured ministers, revealed that she was expecting his child and claimed that Parkinson had promised to leave his wife and marry her. By persuading her minister to stay with his wife, Mrs Thatcher ensured that Sarah Keyes was added to the number of single mothers. Some in government clearly had a 'do as I say not as I do' attitude; in the 1990s it was revealed that Tim Yeo, a government minister and a vociferous opponent of single mothers, had fathered an illegitimate child while still married. Such incidents revealed hypocrisy in, and made a mockery of, the much trumpeted 'Victorian values' and 'back to basics' campaigns.

Although for the majority of women the family was a source of strength and support, in a few cases the reverse was true. The 1976 Domestic Violence Act (see p. 148) had removed the perceived right that a man was entitled to beat his wife, but the Victorian notion that a man had the right to sexual intercourse with his wife remained. This idea was finally removed one hundred years after the Jackson case (see p. 8) had made it illegal for a man to force his wife to live with him. In 1991 the Appeal Court ruled that it was illegal for a man to have sexual intercourse with his wife against her will. If he did so he was guilty of marital rape.

The 'family values' campaign was opposed on more grounds than sexual morality. Many women regarded the attack on benefits as a campaign against the family rather than as support for 'family values'. In particular, wives of miners who were striking to save their industry from closure were incensed by the large cut in benefits paid to strikers. When they found themselves facing real poverty as a result of the long strike and the cut in benefits several of them formed 'Women Against Pit Closures' groups.

It was not unusual for women to be supportive during strikes, but in 1984 they took on a more political role. As well as organising communal feeding they raised funds and several went on speaking tours to gain support. Many who were active during the strike said that they would not be content to return to their former roles once it ended.

Greenham Common peace camp

It was a concern for the future of their families that led a number of women to join the most publicised peace campaign of the century. Although women had been active in peace movements throughout the century, it was the protest at Greenham Common that made the most impact on the public. In August 1981, Ann Pettitt instigated a march from Cardiff to RAF Greenham Common to protest against the siting of 96 American Cruise missiles with nuclear warheads at the base. With the slogan 'Women for life on earth' approximately 40 women, a few with children, and four men, joined her on the 120 mile march. When the group realised that the media showed little or no interest in their protest they made the decision

to camp at the base. Their first action, reminiscent of those of the suffragettes (see p. 21), was to chain themselves to the gates of the base.

In February 1982, the women decided to exclude men from the peace camp. The following December, after an appeal for support, more than 30,000 women from all parts of the country arrived at the camp. They ringed the 16 mile perimeter fence and adorned it with anti-war poems and messages, photographs of children, baby clothes, nappies and teddy bears. As part of their protest, women regularly cut through the perimeter fence and invaded the high-security base. Some danced on the missile silos and others daubed slogans on planes, in the process destroying the effectiveness of the anti-radar paint on them. Many were arrested and taken to court for these activities. Several women, including one quoted in Sue Bruley's *Women in Britain*, argued in court that by their actions they were keeping the peace. Many of the peace protesters, like the suffragettes before them, chose to serve prison sentences rather than pay fines or accept being bound over to keep the peace. They were sent to Holloway but the suffragettes would not have recognised it, as the old prison had been pulled down and rebuilt.

Women at the peace camp.

There were many attempts to evict the women from the site and their caravans and tents were removed. Undaunted, they refused to move and remained on the site living under makeshift shelters. Often they had no more than thin plastic sheeting to protect them from the snow and rain. They had to suffer uncomfortable and unhygienic conditions but they stayed, determined to keep the peace camp going. The population of the camp was not static and the numbers were swelled by women who came to make their protest, sometimes for no more than a couple of days, sometimes for longer. A few stayed for years. The peace camp attracted women from a wide range of backgrounds and from all age groups including many who had not protested before.

Some feminists were uncomfortable about the way that the protesters stressed the differences between men and women in much the same way that the Victorians had. The stereotypes of peace-loving women and war-like men went against the belief that men and women were essentially equal. These assumptions were challenged when Mrs Thatcher went to war over the Falklands. After the ending of the Cold War the missiles were gradually withdrawn but a number of women stayed at the site as a protest against nuclear weapons and to ensure it returned to common land. Although the last Cruise missiles were removed in 1991, the camp was not dismantled until September 2000.

Women in work

While the Greenham women were sitting it out in the peace camp a very different kind of woman was emerging under the influence of Thatcherism. She rejected the radical and socialist ideas of the 1970s women's movement (see p. 139) but, no doubt inspired by seeing a woman lead the country and backed by 1975 Sex Discrimination Act, challenged preconceived ideas about female roles in the workplace. She adopted a more gender-neutral style of dress, hence the power suits, and assailed higher management positions. During this period there was an appreciable increase in the number of women in management, though very few reached the highest levels due to a reluctance of men in the most senior positions to promote them further.

In spite of the 1975 Sex Discrimination Act and the visibility of high-powered women, some stereotypes remained entrenched, and for every enlightened employer there were several whose thinking remained firmly in the past. When Sheila Knight, the editor who commissioned this book, took a second degree in publishing studies in 1990, a tutor advised that her career destiny was to be 'someone's glamorous assistant'. This assumption was echoed by her first employer who surprised her by sending her on a week-long typing course before he even

Dame Anita Roddick OBE (1942–)

Anita Roddick, who founded The Body Shop in 1976 as a way of supporting herself and her children while her husband was away travelling, is an entrepreneur with a difference. She is an outspoken, radical activist who believes in ethical business, something rare enough to have prompted her to call her memoir *Business as Unusual*. Born in 1942 to an Italian immigrant family, she learned about hard work as a child helping out in her family's café in Littlehampton, a small town on the south coast. As she observed in *Business as Unusual*, whereas other cafés in the town opened at 9 a.m. and closed at 5 p.m., her family's café opened at 5 a.m. and did not close until the last customer left.

Although she started The Body Shop with very little capital and no intention other than to earn a livelihood, her vision of creating cosmetics from natural ingredients packaged in simple and refillable containers proved to be popular with customers. Her business flourished but instead of concentrating on increasing profits she used her success to spread her ideas about socially-responsible business. She argued for 'trade not aid' and fought against the exploitation of workers in the Third World. In *Business as Unusual*, she wrote about the importance of women's work in communities across the globe. She believed that profit and principle could work together and became an active campaigner for human rights and the environment. Body Shop customers grew accustomed to finding campaign leaflets and petitions alongside the vitamin E and cocoa butter creams.

Anita Roddick proved her commitment to 'social responsibility' when she made the decision not to leave her large fortune to her children. The bulk of the money that she has made, apart from trust funds and her houses, will go to the The Body Shop Foundation which was founded in 1990 to distribute money to charities. *The Big Issue*, the magazine for the homeless, was one of its early successes. She also helped to found the New Academy for Business which aims to promote values-led business management. Although Anita is no longer co-chairman of The Body Shop, she is an non-executive director and works as a consultant specialising in product development and campaigns.

She recently launched Anita Roddick Publications to help promote human rights and global justice. The first two books, *A Revolution in Kindness* and *Brave Hearts, Rebel Spirits*, were published in June 2003. She was made an OBE in 1988 and a Dame in 2003. She was also nominated for 2003's 'Entrepreneurs' Entrepreneur' award, the results of which will be announced after this book is published.

allocated her a desk. However, she said that these discouragements have been the exception rather than the rule in her career to date.

Although many women were achieving success in the workplace few were receiving equal pay. In 1983 the Government reluctantly complied with a European Community (EC) directive on equal pay for work of equal value and the 1970 Equal Pay Act was strengthened. In 1986, again after pressure from the EC, they strengthened the 1975 Sex Discrimination Act. By the 1980s, the unions were actively committed to equal pay and were involved in many successful cases to implement it. During this period women became more involved with the unions and in 1984 Brenda Dean became the first female union leader.

In sharp contrast to the rise of the executive woman, a large number of working class women found that their working conditions worsened during this period. Under the 1986 Wages Act more than half a million workers lost the protection of the Wages Councils, which regulated wages in several low paid industries. The Government refused to set a minimum wage, and deregulation, and the practice of contracting out work, created more part-time and low paid jobs. While jobs disappeared in heavy industry, more were created in the service industries; this increased the number of jobs for women but they were often low paid. With husbands often out of work the change in working patterns created a great deal of hardship and many women did more than one part-time job. There was also a return to the sweatshops and home-working common in the Victorian period.

It is possible that the scarcity of women in Parliament prevented a toning down of these harsh policies. While Conservative women had some success in protecting child benefit, women in Parliament of all parties were in a weak position. In 1980 there were only 19 women MPs, the lowest number since the early 1950s. In an attempt to change this the 300 club was formed in 1980 to work towards achieving a more equitable number of women MPs. Although the number increased to 60 in the 1991 election, it was clear more needed to be done if women were to make up half of the MPs in parliament. Much of the problem stemmed from constituencies which were reluctant to select women candidates. In order to combat this, the Labour Party introduced positive discrimination in 1993 with all-women short lists. As a result, 101 Labour women were elected in 1997. It is a measure of the attitude of the press that they were immediately nicknamed 'Blair's Babes'.

Girl power and the F-Word

While some women were striving for political power, a very different kind of power was catching the popular imagination in the 1990s. In 1996 the Spice Girls burst onto the scene with their huge number one hit 'Wannabe', and brought the concept of girl power to countless numbers of teenage girls. Their lyrics, which laid down conditions for a man who wanted to be their lover, echoed the words of Mary Quant in the 1960s (see p. 119) who had said that her models were sexy and available but only on their own terms. In other similarities with the 1960s, young women shocked the older generations by the way they dressed. When girls in the 1960s raised their skirts and showed off their legs it was in celebration of freedom from centuries of sexual repression. When girls in the 1990s flaunted their sexuality it was as much a reaction against the 1970s and early 1980s feminism, which they perceived to be anti-men and about wearing frumpy clothes and rejecting make-up.

Although the term 'girl power' had been around for some time, it was the Spice Girls who made it into a catchword for teenage girls. This coincided with the rise in girls' academic success (see box, p. 162). While by no stretch of the imagination could the Spice Girls be seen as academic role models, their very assertiveness and celebration of womanhood would have raised girls' confidence. As much of success depends on psychological attitudes, an increasing sense of their own worth would have helped, especially in mixed schools where girls usually did less well than those in single sex schools.

While the concept of 'girl power' may have given confidence to some, the way in which it was linked by the media and entertainment business to an aggressive sexuality made it anything but empowering for most women. Told that flaunting their bodies gave them power, women soon discovered that this was limited to those whose bodies conformed to an ideal. As a result, many whose bodies failed to match up became insecure. A growing number of women, Princess Diana among them, and some barely teenagers, fell victim to the eating disorders anorexia and bulimia. Women also came under increasing pressure to undergo surgery to conform to an ideal. I knew of a young woman who asked her parents for liposuction for her eighteenth birthday.

The idea that a woman was empowered by using her sexuality was very much a late twentieth idea, although it is not far removed from the views of the anti-suffragist Marie Corelli (see p. 23). She used different words but she too believed that women had all the power they needed through their femininity. As 'feminine wiles' was just a euphemism for sexual power there is little difference in the concept. However, as countless women discovered, the use of feminine wiles or blatant sexuality alone does not bring a woman respect – nor does it bring equal pay and equal opportunities.

A new generation of feminists emerged during the early 1990s, partly influenced by the 'riot grrl' movement which had started in music but spread into

The 'Hermione' factor – girls and education

It is unlikely that J. K. Rowling could have created Hermione Granger, the clever and studious friend of Harry Potter, before the 1990s without making her into some kind of oddity. The remarkable feature about Hermione is not that she is clever but that the boys have no problem in accepting her superior academic success. In the past intelligent women were regarded with suspicion and taught to hide their intelligence if they wanted to be accepted by men. As late as the early 1960s one university student was told by her fiancé that, while he would be happy if she equalled his result, if she did any better their engagement was off.

By the 1990s, however, it had not only become acceptable for a girl to be studious, it was becoming the norm. In response to demands for equal opportunities in education from the women's movement, by the 1980s most Local Authorities had created equal opportunities initiatives in their schools. The outcome was that girls' results steadily improved, and by the end of the 1990s girls were making headlines by out-performing boys in almost every subject. Hermione's success lies in the fact that she works hard both in and out of the classroom, but rather than seeing studying as a chore she is shown to enjoy it. The enormous popularity of the Harry Potter books and films means that the countless number of young girls who identify with Hermione are getting the message that studying is 'cool'. It is quite likely that the 'Hermione factor' could boost the number of girls striving to do well at school.

other areas. Women associated with riot grrls had their own bands, published their own fanzines, started their own record labels and were involved in political protests. The lyrics of girl bands in the riot grrl movement were highly political. In comparison, the 'girl power' of the Spice Girls was tame in the extreme. At the end of the twentieth century and the beginning of the twenty-first, young feminists began to reject the commercialisation of their bodies in much the same way that the 1970s feminists reacted against the exploitation of women in the 1960s. The younger feminists, however, were living in a different era and had a different agenda. In the 1990s they also faced the problem that many believed the battle had been won and feminism was therefore out-dated and irrelevant. Recognising this prejudice against even the word 'feminism', one group of feminists named their website 'the F-Word'.

Having it all?

By the last two decades of the century women were faced with an array of choices that would have seemed impossible to those born at the start of the century. They had a bewildering range of careers; they could choose whether to marry or stay single and whether or not to have children. If they chose motherhood they could choose whether or not to stay at home, as either their man or the state would support them. They were also free to make multi-choices. They no longer had to decide between a career or marriage or even a career and motherhood. It seemed that they could have anything that they really wanted, making some believe that they could defy the proverb and both have their cake and eat it.

The reality of course was somewhat different. Unless a woman had a great deal of money 'having it all' meant a great deal of extra work. Even when women paid half of all household expenses, it was rare for a husband or partner to undertake half the responsibility of looking after a home and children. Mrs Thatcher had a demanding career as well as two children, but she had a rich, supportive husband and could afford nannies and housekeepers. Nicola Horlick, one of the city's high-flyers, was acclaimed as a 'superwoman' because she also had a large family. In an interview for the BBC online news she rejected the description, pointing out that she had a nanny and secretary and that ordinary women who had jobs and ran their families without help were the ones who deserved to be called 'superwomen'.

Some women came to the conclusion that it was not possible to have it all, and chose their careers over having children. A few postponed starting a family and found that they had left it too late. Others decided to opt out of work until their children started school. For stay-at-home mothers the problem of 'cabbagehood' referred to in the 1960s chapter remained a problem. Many felt isolated and though reluctant to admit it many were bored. Even mixing with other mothers did not always help them as the talk usually centred on children and related subjects. It was even harder for women who had given up rewarding and enjoyable jobs. For many, the greatest difficulty was the loss of contact with the wider world.

One woman confided that she had felt very guilty at the thought of putting her one-year-old child in a nursery for half a day, but she had felt she would go mad without some time to herself. She was living away from her family and spent most of the day alone with her son. In the past she would probably have been able to have some time for herself by leaving her child with a neighbour, aunt or grandmother. However the changes in women's lives have meant that, more likely than not, neighbours and aunts are working and a grandmother too is likely to have a career of her own. Even those who have retired may not be available for child-minding duties. Retired women who were young in the 1960s and 1970s are more likely to be busy with clubs or committees, embarking on a new course of study, or off travelling the world.

While 'having it all' was an impossible dream for most women in the 1990s, the very fact that it was being spoken of at all shows how far women's lives had changed since the century began. For all the difficulties that they faced at the end of the twentieth century few women would have wished to change places with their great-grandmothers at the start of it.

Baroness Patricia Scotland QC (1955–)

Patricia Scotland, who became a peer in 1997 when she was created Baroness Scotland of Asthal, was born in Dominica in 1955. One of 12 children, she came to England when she was a small child. She was educated at London University where she read law and where, according to a report in the *Guardian* in June 2001, a lecturer warned her that that being black and female 'might be too big a hurdle to overcome'. She was to prove the lecturer wrong and was called to the bar in 1977. As a barrister she specialised in family law until 1991 when, at the very young age of 35, she became the first black woman QC. She served on the Commission for Racial Equality and from 1994–9 was a member of the Millennium Commission.

At one point it was thought that she would become the first black woman High Court judge, but when Labour came to power she was made a life peer. In 1999, she became Britain's first

black female government minister when she was appointed to the Foreign and Commonwealth Office. She proved to be a good minister and was moved to the Lord Chancellor's department in 2001. She is currently a minister of state in the Home Office.

Her achievement in becoming the first black woman QC was widely reported. Her success was an inspiration to a number of black girls in the school where I taught, especially those considering a career in law. In 1991 it was a pleasant change for them to see a black woman making a success in a career dominated by white males.

Milestones

1901	Death of Queen Victoria
1903	Mrs Pankhurst founds the Women's Social and Political Union (WSPU)
1905	First suffragettes imprisoned (Christabel Pankhurst and Annie Kenney)
1911	Census boycott
1913	Emily Davison, suffragette, killed at the Derby
1913	Prisoners' (Temporary Discharge for Ill-health) Act (known as the 'Cat and Mouse Act')
1914–18	First World War
	Suffrage campaign halted for the duration of the war
	Women join women's auxiliary services and do other war work
1918	Vote granted to women over 30
	Women allowed to stand for Parliament
	Maternity and Child Welfare Act
	Married Love and *Wise Parenthood* published
	Constance Markievicz (Sinn Fein) only woman elected in general election
1919	Lady Nancy Astor becomes first woman to sit in the House of Commons
1921	Marie Stopes opens first birth control clinic in Holloway, London
1923	Marriage Act gives women the right to divorce on the same grounds as men
	Five women elected to parliament
1924	Margaret Bondfield becomes the first woman in government
1926	Equal Rights procession in Hyde Park
1928	Women granted the vote on the same terms as men.
1930	Amy Johnson becomes the first woman to fly solo from England to Australia
1936	'Red' Ellen Wilkinson MP accompanies the Jarrow March
1938	Government sets up the Women's Voluntary Service (WVS) and Women's Land Army
1939	Family Planning Association set up

Housewives! **W·V·S** *needs your help!*
Even if tied to your home you can help the wardens and your neighbours
DON'T DELAY...ENQUIRE TO-DAY

1939–45	Second World War
1941	Women conscripted for war work
1946	Royal Commission on Equal Pay
	Civil service ends its marriage bar
1952	London County Council awards equal pay to some of its staff
1953	Queen Elizabeth II's coronation
1955	Teachers, civil servants and local government officers granted equal pay
1959	Margaret Thatcher elected MP for Finchley
1963	Women who were peeresses in their own right allowed to sit in the Lords
1964	Seven women appointed to government posts by Harold Wilson
1965	Elizabeth Lane becomes the first woman High Court judge
1967	Abortion legalised
1969	Divorce reform makes breakdown of marriage only grounds for divorce
1970	Equal Pay Act
1971	Erin Pizzey opens first refuge for battered women
1975	Sex Discrimination Act
	Margaret Thatcher becomes first woman to lead a British political party
1976	Nobel Peace Prize awarded to Mairead Corrigan and Betty Williams
1979	Margaret Thatcher becomes Britain's first woman Prime Minister
1981	Greenham Common women's peace camp set up
1986	Sex Discrimination Act
1987	Diane Abbott, Britain's first black woman MP, elected
1990	Women allowed to serve on warships
1991	RAF allows women to train as fighter pilots
1994	First women priests ordained in the Church of England
1997	119 women elected as MPs
2000	24-year-old Ellen MacArthur sets off to sail in the Vendée Globe, a single-handed race round the world

Further reading

Arthur, Max, *Forgotten Voices of the Great War* (Ebury Press, 2002)

Binney, Marcus, *Women Who Lived for Danger: The Woman Agents of SOE in the Second World War* (Hodder and Stoughton, 2002)

Bird, Isabella, *A Lady's Life in the Rocky Mountains* (Virago, 1991)

Brittain, Vera, *Chronicle of Youth* (Phoenix Press, 2000)

Brittain, Vera, *Testament of Youth: An Autobiographical Study of the Years 1900–1925* (Virago Modern Classics, 2001)

Bruley, Sue, *Women in Britain Since 1900* (Palgrave, 1999)

Forrester, Helen, *Twopence to Cross the Mersey* (Harper Collins, 1995)

Forrester, Helen, *Lime Street at Two* (Harper Collins, 1994)

Holdsworth, Angela. *Out of the Doll's House: The Story of Women in the Twentieth Century* (BBC Books, 1988)

Lawrence, Dorothy, *Sapper Dorothy Lawrence: The Only English Woman Soldier* (John Lane, the Bodley Head, 1919)

Lively, Penelope, *A House Unlocked* (Penguin Books, 2001)

Luff, David, *Amy Johnson: Enigma in the Sky* (Airlife, 2002)

Lytton, Lady Constance, *Prisons and Prisoners: Some Personal Experiences* (Virago, 1988)

Mackenzie, Midge, *Shoulder to Shoulder: A Documentary* (Allen Lane, 1975)

Marlow, Joyce (ed.), *Votes for Women: The Virago Book of Suffragettes* (Virago, 2001)

Marlow, Joyce (ed.), *The Virago Book of Women and the Great War, 1914–18* (Virago, 1998)

Mayer, Annette, *Women in Britain, 1900–2000* (Hodder and Stoughton, 2002)

Murray, Jenni, *The Woman's Hour* (BBC Books, 1996)

Pankhurst, Emmeline, *My Own Story* (Virago, 1979)

Pizzey, Erin, *Infernal Child* (Gollancz, 1978)

Pizzey, Erin, *Scream Quietly or the Neighbours Will Hear* (Penguin, 1974)

Pizzey, Erin, and Shapiro, Jeff, *Prone to Violence* (Hamlyn, 1982)

Pollock, Mary, *Family Planning Today* (New English Library, 1963)

Pugh, Martin, *Women and the Women's Movement in Britain 1914–1999* (Macmillan, 2000)

Raeburn, Antonia, *The Militant Suffragettes* (Michael Joseph, 1973)

Roddick, Anita, *Business as Unusual* (Thorsons, 2000)

Rowbotham, Sheila, *A Century of Women: The History of Women in Britain and the United States* (Penguin, 1999)

Sayre, Anne, *Rosalind Franklin and DNA* (Norton, 1975)

Seacole, Mary, *Wonderful Adventures of Mrs Seacole in Many Lands* (X Press, 1999)

Septima, *Something to Do* (Penguin, 1966)

Septima, *What's on for Children (and Young People)* (Periodical Publications, 1961)

Sebba, Anne, *Battling for the News* (Hodder and Stoughton, 1995)

Sheridan, Dorothy (ed.), *Wartime Women: An Anthology of Women's Wartime Writing for Mass-observation 1937–45* (Phoenix Press, 2000)

Stack, Mary Bagot, *Building the Body Beautiful: the Bagot Stack Stretch-and-swing System* (Chapman and Hall, 1931)

Stopes, Marie, *Married Love: A New Contribution to the Solution of Sex Difficulties* (Gollancz, 1995)

Stopes, Marie, *Wise Parenthood: A Treatise on Birth Control for Married People* (Putnam, 1947)

Stott, Mary, *Forgetting's No Excuse* (Virago, 1989)

Stott, Mary, *Before I Go: Reflections on My Life and Times* (Virago, 1985)

Watson, James, *The Double Helix: A Personal Account of the Discovery of DNA* (Penguin, 1999)

Weldon, Fay, *Auto da Fay* (Flamingo, 2002)

Wilkinson, Ellen, *The Town That Was Murdered* (Left Book Club, 1939)

Picture sources

All document references are to holdings of the National Archives: Public Record Office unless stated otherwise.

Jacket **front** Mary Evans Picture Library **front thumbnails** COPY 1/494, photograph by Frank Clarke; Maureen Geary-Andrews; © Tim Graham/CORBIS **back** RAIL 393/174 **left flap** NATS 1/1307 **right flap** © Trish Anderson

Prelims **iii** Gene Shelley **vi** INF 13/117

A woman's place **2** COPY 1/424, photograph by Alexander Bassano **4** *A Lady's Life in the Rocky Mountains* by Isabella L. Bird (John Murray, 1879) **5** COPY 1/409 **7** *Caroline Norton* by Alice Acland (Constable, 1948) **11** ZPER 34/102, *The Illustrated London News* **12–13** COPY 1/445, photograph by Thomas Taylor

Deeds not words **16** COPY 1/494 **18** COPY 1/526 **22** Mary Evans Picture Library/The Women's Library **25** HO 144/1052 **27** Mary Evans Picture Library/The Women's Library, photograph by Lena Connell **29** Mary Evans Picture Library, artist A. Pearse **30** COPY 1/551, photograph by Victor Console **32** AR 1/528, Wallace Collection

On her their lives depend **34** © Hulton-Deutsch Collection/CORBIS **37** RAIL 343/725 **39** MUN 5/164/1124/40 **40** MAF 59/3 **42** *La Vie et la Mort de Miss Edith Cavell* (Fontemoing, 1915) **44** Betty Storey **47** Mary Evans Picture Library, photograph by Harris in *Good Housekeeping*

The 'modern miss' **50** Robert Pols, photograph by Charles Howell **52** RAIL 393/174 **53** Mary Turner **56** Mary Evans Picture Library **57** LAB 2/1589 **59** Mary Turner **62** Mary Evans Picture Library/The Women's Library **64** © Hulton-Deutsch Collection/CORBIS

Domestic bliss or suburban neurosis? **66** © Hulton-Deutsch Collection/CORBIS **68** © Hulton-Deutsch Collection/CORBIS **70** © Hulton-Deutsch Collection/CORBIS **74** CO 956/178, artist Frank Newbould **77** HO 45/17040 **79** © Hulton-Deutsch Collection/CORBIS

What did you do in the war, mummy? **82** © Hulton-Deutsch Collection/CORBIS **85** LAB 44/252 **86** INF 2/44 **89** HS 9/1435 **91** INF 3/400 **92** Betty Storey **94** MAF 223/21 **96** © Hulton-Deutsch Collection/CORBIS **99** © Hulton-Deutsch Collection/CORBIS

From Housewives Choice to rock and roll **100** © H. Armstrong Roberts/CORBIS **102** Joan Huggins **105** Mary Turner **106** Girton College, University of Cambridge **110** © Hulton-Deutsch Collection/CORBIS **112** © Hulton-Deutsch Collection/CORBIS **115** © Bettmann/CORBIS **116** Henry Grant Collection/Museum of London

Dolly birds and double standards **118** COAL 80/1119 **119** © John Springer Collection/CORBIS **120** Mary Evans Picture Library/AD LIB Studios **122** MEPO 13/60 **125** George Knight **126** © Jane Brown **131** © Bettmann/CORBIS **133** © Hulton-Deutsch Collection/CORBIS

Feminists or free spirits? **134** © Bettmann/CORBIS **137** Mary Evans Picture Library **139** © Hulton-Deutsch Collection/CORBIS **140** The Advertising Archives/*Spare Rib* **142** © Hulton-Deutsch Collection/CORBIS **147** © Hulton-Deutsch Collection/ CORBIS

Having it all? **150 left** © Bettmann/CORBIS **150 right** © Graham Tim/CORBIS SYGMA **153** © Nick Sinclair/CORBIS **154** © Hulton-Deutsch Collection/CORBIS **157** © Caroline Penn/CORBIS **159** © Hulton-Deutsch Collection/CORBIS **164** © The Guardian, photograph by Martin Argles

Milestones **165** INF 13/214

Index